STEAM LOCOMOTIVES 1955

70000 – 90774

STANDARDS AND AUSTERITIES

During the fifties there was only one regular express duty on the East Coast main line south of Peterborough worked by B1 class locomotives. This was the Cleethorpes–Kings Cross service hauled by Immingham depot engines. In the early sixties these were replaced by 'Britannias', which had formerly worked Great Eastern services. Here, no. 70040 *Clive of India* is seen leaving Huntingdon. The reign of the 'Britannias' was short-lived, and they were soon replaced by diesels. *Clive of India* was transferred to Carlisle for the rest of its working days.

24.8.61

STEAM LOCOMOTIVES 1955

70000 – 90774

STANDARDS AND AUSTERITIES

ERIC SAWFORD

SUTTON PUBLISHING

First published in the United Kingdom in 1998
Sutton Publishing Limited · Phoenix Mill
Thrupp · Stroud · Gloucestershire · GL5 2BU

British Library Cataloguing in Publication Data
A catalogue record for this book is available from the British Library

ISBN 0-7509-1617-6

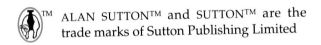 ™ ALAN SUTTON™ and SUTTON™ are the
trade marks of Sutton Publishing Limited

Typeset in 10/12pt Palatino.
Typesetting and origination by
Sutton Publishing Limited.
Printed in Great Britain by
Butler & Tanner, Frome, Somerset.

Contents

With the arrival of 'Britannias' in March, I made several visits at weekends to photograph these fine engines, especially those still in traffic and not stored in the yard. No. 70009 *Alfred the Great* was in an excellent position for photography in the shed yard.

26.5.63

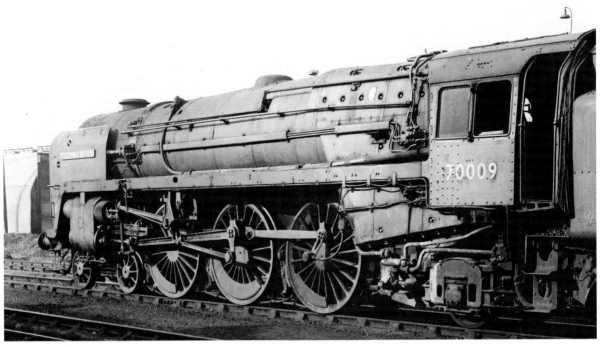

Another shot of no. 70009 *Alfred the Great*. Seven months after this picture was taken, the engine was moved to Carlisle Kingmoor where it remained in service until January 1967, ending its days at McWilliams scrapyard, Shettleston, five months later.

26.5.63

Introduction

Following nationalisation in 1948 and the announcement of a new range of BR Standard designs, it was with considerable interest that the first locomotive, no. 70000 *Britannia*, was awaited. Completed at Crewe Works in January 1951, this engine appeared in black livery and it ran extensive trials before returning to Crewe to be repainted in Brunswick Green fully lined livery. It was officially named by the then Minister of Transport on 20 January 1951 at Marylebone station.

My first sighting of a 'Britannia' was at the 1951 Festival of Britain held at the South Bank site in London. No. 70004 *William Shakespeare* had gone there straight from Crewe Works and, as might be imagined, it had been given special treatment at the works and by cleaners on site before the exhibition opened. The engine remained on display from April to September, but unfortunately I was unable to photograph it there. *William Shakespeare* was later allocated to the Southern Region where, in company with no. 70014 *Iron Duke* it worked the prestigious 'Golden Arrow' and 'Night Ferry' services.

The first opportunity I had to photograph a 'Britannia' was at Old Oak Common depot. No. 70017 *Arrow*, at the time just a few months old, was in the shed yard, being one of several engines allocated there. These locomotives were not particularly well received by enginemen used to Great Western designs such as 'Kings', 'Castles' and 'Halls' on express passenger services.

However, the class was eventually to become fifty-five strong. The initial batch was allocated to the Great Eastern Section, with examples going to Stratford and Norwich depots. There was at the time an urgent need for new motive power on this line, and the 'Britannias' soon proved themselves. Regular interval services between Liverpool Street and Norwich were introduced on 2 July 1951 and the 'Britannias' were well up to the new faster services. These engines also worked into Cambridge where I was able to record on film several members of the class in their very early years. Eventually they were to be found on all regions. The East Coast main line was well served by Gresley and other Pacifics, but in the early sixties one duty resulted in an Immingham 'Britannia' working through to Kings Cross on the Cleethorpes service and the return train in the early evening. Prior to the allocation of 'Britannias' to Immingham, these being replaced on the Great Eastern service by diesels, the Kings Cross–Cleethorpes service had been worked by immaculate B1s. This train ran non-stop from Peterborough to Kings Cross, while the return service, also on a fast timing, made its first stop at Huntingdon. Immediately after leaving the station the long 1 in 200 climb to Abbots Ripton commences, and while this presented few problems to the B1s, the more powerful Britannias, with their 6 ft 2 in driving wheels, simply roared away. But time was already running out for steam on the East Coast main line, and I was fortunate to record several members of the class on film.

In September 1961 I was very surprised by the appearance of *Britannia* itself at Huntingdon on a northbound fast goods. Only three months previously this engine had

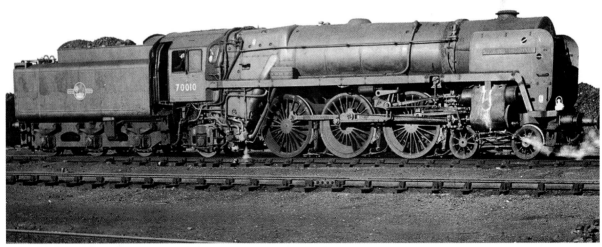

A great many pictures were taken of 'Britannias' in their working days but only seldom does one see an almost broadside view which illustrates clearly the 68 ft 9 in overall length of the engine and tender. No. 70010 *Owen Glendower* was photographed at March having been transferred there when diesels took over the Great Eastern services. After leaving March in March 1963 it went to Willesden until January 1965 when it was transferred to Crewe, ending its days at Carlisle in September 1967.

9.9.62

been transferred to March depot along with other members of the class. Just why it turned up on this duty I never found out. March engines were extremely rare on the main line south of Peterborough, and I was expecting the usual V2 class 2–6–2, so the appearance of *Britannia* took me rather by surprise. However, I was able to record the moment on film, and the picture appears in this book.

As already mentioned, several displaced Britannias were sent to March; some were to find work, others were placed in store in various parts of the yard. The depot itself was, by this time, in decline. As at other Eastern Region depots, at March the chimneys of stored engines were always covered with a piece of tarpaulin. Only a handful of 'Britannias' were to remain in regular service while at the shed. With steam locomotives being rapidly withdrawn, it looked as though some 'Britannias' would not see further service. At this time there were many engines of several classes in store at March; these included some already withdrawn and awaiting their final journey to the scrapyard. Fortunately this was not the case with the 'Britannias', as they were reallocated in 1963, mostly to Carlisle Kingmoor, and returned to traffic. Looking back it is remarkable that most, if not all, the March engines still carried their nameplates while in store. In later years it was very different, and I photographed several with no front number or nameplates; the name was sometimes painted or even chalked on, or was non-existent. In addition to this, these engines were often in a terrible external condition.

There were, of course, exceptions. No. 70013 *Oliver Cromwell* was used on many rail tours following its last general overhaul at Crewe Works. It was the last steam locomotive overhauled for British Railways, emerging from the works fully repainted; the occasion was marked by a ceremony on 2 February 1967 before the engine returned to traffic. *Oliver Cromwell* had been chosen for preservation in preference to *Britannia* itself which had been vandalised while in store. Following its overhaul, *Oliver Cromwell* was extensively used on specials, its final working taking place over the Settle and Carlisle line. Immediately afterwards it set out under its own steam for its new home at the Steam Museum at Bressingham, travelling via Doncaster to Norwich; here it was prepared for towing to Diss, the final part of the journey being made by road. The engine arrived on 16 August 1968 and has remained at Bressingham ever since. For a number of years it was regularly in steam at the museum.

Britannia, the engine originally chosen for the National Collection, has also survived. Withdrawn in June 1966 it was sent to Stratford Works for storage, later being moved to Preston Park (Brighton). It was eventually purchased and moved to the Severn Valley Railway in 1971, and since then it has had several homes and has been seen in many parts of the country (sometimes masquerading as other long-since departed members of the class). During its BR days *Britannia* had seen service from several depots; when new, it had been allocated to Stratford where it was the Royal Train engine. On 11 February 1952 it worked the Royal Train conveying the body of King George VI from King's Lynn to Kings Cross for lying in state at Westminster Hall. When diesels replaced the 'Britannias' on the Great Eastern section, *Britannia*, which had been transferred to Norwich in 1961, was sent to March and was eventually placed in store; it was transferred to the London Midland Region in March 1963, and its final shed in BR service was Newton Heath. Over the years I have photographed both the surviving engines on numerous occasions.

The arrival of the Standard classes coincided with my purchasing a decent camera so I was able to record these engines throughout their short working lives and also photographed several as they awaited their fate in scrapyards. Initially it was generally thought that these engines would have long active working lives, and few people imagined, when *Britannia* appeared in 1951, that all the class would be withdrawn just seventeen years later. The working life of Standard 9F *Evening Star*, completed at Swindon in March 1960, was much shorter, as it was for most other members of that class, as steam ended on normal revenue-earning service on British Railways in August 1968.

My first real opportunity to photograph examples of the Standard class 5s came at Derby Works in 1953, the design having been introduced in 1951. Most of them were built at Derby, with some being built at Doncaster from 1955. At the time of my visit in 1953, no. 73032 was new on the shed yard, together with no. 73031, which was one of two delivered with a Westinghouse pump fitted for freight train trials. In 1956 the first of the Caprotti valve gear locomotives was completed. Following hard on the heels of the Stanier class 5s the Standards soon proved themselves popular with the engine crews; they were reliable, powerful locomotives which could handle heavy trains. This was also true of the Caprottis, which were highly regarded for their haulage capabilities.

In time Standard 5s were to be found on all regions, and the last examples in service in 1968 were often requested for enthusiasts specials. The Southern Region allocated names previously carried by 'King Arthurs' to twenty of the Standard class 5s. They all had new plates, mounted on the side of the running plate. As diesels took over more and more duties, some of the Standard class 5 locomotives in their later years were to be seen on carriage pilot duties in and out of Waterloo, often in a very work-stained condition.

Standard class 5s were not generally to be seen on the East Coast main line south of Peterborough although Kings Cross received no. 73071 on loan in 1956, and it was frequently used on Cambridge services. It is recorded that it also worked to Hull, although I did not see it. With the completion of the final batch at Doncaster in 1957 the

The versatile lightweight 4–6–0s of the 75000 series soon proved themselves ideal locomotives on cross-country routes. Here, no. 75036, one of several allocated to Bletchley shed, awaits its next duty. These engines and the 80000 series 2–6–4Ts were extensively used on the Cambridge services.

15.7.54

class totalled 172 locomotives. Withdrawals commenced in 1964, leaving no. 73069 as the last in service. This engine, together with no. 73040, as already mentioned, was often seen on specials in the last months, but neither was to survive into preservation.

In the early fifties many secondary lines were worked by elderly engines. The year 1951 was very interesting, with five of the new Standard designs appearing. One was the first of the class 4 lightweight 4–6–0s of the 75000 series built at Swindon. These were a versatile design, the low axle loading permitting access to places where larger engines were prohibited, while the fact that they were tender locomotives gave them a longer working range. In a short time they were to be seen on many routes, among them the Bletchley–Cambridge service which they took over from Stanier 4MTs. Another depot to receive an early allocation of these locomotives was Bedford, which had operated Compounds on the St Pancras local trains; the class 4s soon proved popular, as did the Standard 4MT tanks which were also to be found there at the time. In all eighty were built, all at Swindon, between 1951 and 1957; there were plans for a further batch but this was cancelled. In due course a number of these engines were fitted with double blastpipes and chimneys to improve their performance.

Another design to appear in 1951 was the 'Clan' class 6 Pacific; these fell short of expectations, the Standard 5 class proving to be almost equal in performance. All ten 'Clans' were built at Crewe; there were plans for a further fifteen but these were never constructed. The 'Clans' were allocated to Polmadie and Carlisle Kingmoor, both at the time of construction being included in the Scottish Region. Their duties often took them south of the border on trains to Liverpool, Manchester and Leeds. The first five of the class were condemned in 1962, and four of those remaining were withdrawn in 1965. The last example, no. 72008 *Clan MacLeod*, was withdrawn in 1966. None has survived.

The first of the Standard 4MT 2–6–4Ts were also built at Derby. Developed from the very popular Fairburn design, these were powerful locomotives having good acceleration and capable of a good turn of speed; they were widely used in their early days on suburban and local passenger duties. Construction was mostly at Brighton; some were also built at Derby and Doncaster. The last example was completed in 1956, bringing the class to its full strength of 155 locomotives. These engines were originally allocated to all regions except the Western, although they were to be found here also in later years.

As with so many of the Standard locomotives they were replaced by diesels and multiple diesel units, and often found themselves relegated to more mundane duties. One such example, on the Southern, worked empty stock into and out of Waterloo, often in company with Standard class 5s, on what was for many years the domain of M7 class 0–4–4Ts until the early sixties.

In 1952 a very useful 2–6–0, the 76000 class, appeared from Horwich. These were basically the well-liked Ivatt 2–6–0 introduced in 1947, with standard details incorporated; the designers also took the opportunity to improve the appearance generally. In all 115 were built between 1952 and 1957 at Horwich and Doncaster, the final example being the last steam locomotive to be built by Doncaster. Withdrawals commenced in 1964, with the last going in 1967; four have survived the scrapman's cutting torch.

Also included in my early railway photographs were the very versatile Ivatt lightweight 2–6–0s of the 6400 class which were introduced in 1946. These were designed to take over duties which were then in the hands of elderly locomotives rapidly approaching the end of their working lives on cross-country and secondary lines. One such was the Kettering–Cambridge service worked by ex-Midland 2F 0–6–0s. This was a rather steeply graded line at the Northamptonshire end and the 2Fs with their open and rather spartan cabs must have been far from suitable in the winter time. The Ivatt engines with their many improvements, principal among these a comfortable cab, were warmly welcomed by Kettering locomotive crews. Initially the first five engines of the class were allocated for these duties, and three more followed in due course, with nos 78020/1 of the Standard class 2MTs introduced in 1952 arriving later.

These new engines were in effect the Ivatt design modified to the new Standard specifications. The class was already well proven, reliable, economical and well thought out, their size and low axle loading making them useful for a great many applications. Indeed the original Ivatt engines were still being built well into nationalisation. All sixty-five examples of the Standard 2MTs were built at Darlington between 1952 and 1956. In 1956 I was fortunate to see and photograph several examples of the final batch under construction; they were at various stages, with no. 78056 almost complete. This particular batch was destined for London Midland Region depots. These lightweight 2–6–0s are ideal engines for many preserved lines and in total ten have survived, the majority of which are of the original Ivatt design.

The Standard class 4MT 2–6–4Ts were designed at Brighton with the benefit of a long experience of locomotives of this wheel arrangement. No. 80066 was constructed at Brighton in 1953 and is seen here at Bletchley depot; these engines worked local passenger services to Euston as well as cross-country services.

15.7.54

When the Standards were being planned it became apparent that a tank design of class 3 was required, suitable for lines with axle loading restrictions which prohibited the class 4 2–6–4Ts but at the same time more powerful than the class 2s. In 1952 the first example of this design, the 82000 series, was out-shopped from Swindon; although considerably more were originally planned the final production figure was forty-five. A successful design, these engines were ideal for the duties intended, but they were victims of circumstance as improvements to track and other civil engineering work upgraded many of the routes, thus enabling larger engines to be used; together with the introduction of diesel multiple units, this considerably reduced their workings.

In their final years examples of the class were widespread, and they could be found working on the Somerset & Dorset, as well as on carriage pilot duties in and out of Waterloo. Some of the latter were engines which had spent much of their working lives in the north-east. Withdrawals commenced in 1964, and sadly none survived into preservation. Several which finished their days on the Southern Region working in the London area were to end up at Cohens scrapyard, Kettering, as did some of the W class 2–6–4Ts which had a long association with Hither Green depot, where they were often seen on inter-regional goods workings.

In the same year (1946) that Ivatt introduced his lightweight 2–6–0s, the 2–6–2 passenger tank version made its appearance. Another very successful design, they were efficient, powerful and easy to maintain, at the same time having a wide route availability. These engines were built right up to 1952. The following year the first of the Standard class 2 2–6–2Ts emerged from Crewe Works; as with the tender engines, these were basically the same design although with slight modifications and BR fittings. The original batch, nos 84000–19, all went to London Midland Region depots. In 1957 Darlington built another ten. As with many other steam locomotives the railways modernisation programme resulted in many duties being taken over by diesels. By the early sixties examples of these and the Ivatt engines were to be found in store; although the first was not withdrawn until 1963, by the end of 1965 all had been condemned, with none surviving into preservation.

At the start of 1954 two of the planned Standard designs still had to make their appearance: the class 3 mixed traffic 2–6–0s of the 77000 series and the long-awaited heavy goods locomotives, the 9F 2–10–0s. There was also one other very important locomotive still to make its debut: the 8P Pacific no. 71000 *Duke of Gloucester*. This was in fact a special authorisation, principally because of the loss of the London Midland Region Pacific no. 46202 *Princess Anne* in the Harrow & Wealdstone crash in 1952, which left the region one Pacific short.

Although a large 4–6–2 design had been introduced in the original planning it had been left in abeyance as it was thought that sufficient large Pacifics were available; only a limited amount of design work was in fact carried out, and this was based on the well-known LMS 'Duchess' class. Built at Crewe, the *Duke of Gloucester* was very different to the 'Duchess' class, being fitted with Caprotti valve gear. It was to spend most of its life allocated to Crewe North shed but experienced persistent steaming difficulties. Some modifications were made in 1961 which improving the situation, but this was too late, as by then diesels were appearing in considerable numbers and taking over express duties. In November 1962 no. 71000 was withdrawn; originally listed for preservation as part of the National Collection, it was stored at Crewe North depot and later Crewe Works. Later in the sixties it was decided to preserve only the left-hand-side cylinder and valve gear, although the other side was also removed, the engine standing in Crewe Works yard in a very sad state awaiting disposal. Sold for scrap to Woodhams of Barry it was first delivered in error to J. Cashmores of Newport, before being sent on to Barry. Had this not happened it would certainly not be with us today. It was to spend over seven years exposed to the elements before being rescued. Restoration to working order proved to be a mammoth undertaking, and new external cylinders were among the new items required. In the process many improvements have been made, resulting in a vastly improved performance by this fine locomotive.

In 1954 Swindon Works completed the first class 3 of the 77000 series. These were tender versions of the 82000 2–6–2Ts tanks, and only twenty were built, going to depots in the North Eastern and Scottish Regions. Only one was to venture south: no. 77014 was sent to Guildford from the London Midland Region in early 1966. It was to remain here until withdrawal in July 1967, this rendering the class extinct.

It fell to Crewe to build the first example of the final Standard class, the 9F 2–10–0 heavy goods locomotives. Certainly one of the most successful of all the Standards, these powerful engines experienced some braking problems. New England depot received 9Fs fairly soon after they were introduced, and owing to the braking problem, trials were conducted at several points on the East Coast main line, one point being at Huntingdon. For some distance, Up trains were on a falling gradient of 1 in 200, added to which

Standard class 9F no. 92008 was one of the original batch built at Crewe in 1954. It is seen here at its home shed, Wellingborough. These locomotives soon replaced the Beyer-Garratts on the Midland main line. The 9Fs and class 8F 2–8–0s monopolised the heavy mineral trains right up to the end of steam working. Note the whistle sign and restricted clearance of the shed entrance.

27.3.55

immediately after the station most goods trains were turned 'slow road', and by this time, after several miles of 'one up line' from Abbots Ripton, quite often express trains would be held up behind them. Braking problems had been encountered previously, especially with the Little Barford power station coal trains, and so ex-Great Central L3 class 2–6–4T no. 69064 was transferred to work this duty; however, this was short-lived and the L3 was soon sent back to its original depot, the duty reverting to an ex-WD Austerity 2–8–0. Once the braking problems were solved the 9Fs became very popular and were to be seen on this section of the East Coast main line right up to the end of steam working.

Ten 9F locomotives, nos 92020–9, were built with a Franco-Crosti boiler at Crewe in 1955. These were thought to be economical in terms of coal consumption, but this was not the case as they did not come up to expectations; coupled with high maintenance requirements and corrosion problems, just three years later most were out of use. In due course all were rebuilt, but still retaining their smaller boiler and firebox. The Crostis were based at Wellingborough depot; after modification some remained in the area while others went to more distant sheds.

The 9F locomotives also underwent several other experiments, such as the fitting of Giesel exhaust systems and mechanical stokers. Several 9Fs were fitted with Westinghouse pumps to operate hopper doors on the Consett iron ore trains, a demanding duty on this steeply graded line, taking over from 01 2–8–0s and Q7 0–8–0s. In all 251 locomotives were built, with the last, no. 92220 *Evening Star* having the double distinction of being the last steam locomotive built at Swindon and the last delivered to British Railways. The engine was fitted with Great Western-type copper cap double chimney and turned out in full British Railways fully lined passenger green livery, the naming ceremony taking place at Swindon Works. Scheduled for preservation from the

For a great many years the principal heavy goods locomotive of the London Midland Region was Stanier's workhorse, the 8F 2–8–0. The considerable number of WD 2–8–0s to be found in the north were joined in 1954 by the 9F 2–10–0. Time was rapidly running out for steam when this picture was taken at March in 1965; 8F no. 48600 and WD no. 90401 were both visitors.

7.2.65

onset, this engine was to have the shortest working life of any of the standards, being withdrawn from Cardiff East Dock shed in March 1965, exactly five years after completion.

Several members of the class were to end their days at Barry, from where they have been rescued for preservation. *Evening Star* itself was to see further service on specials and preserved lines before returning to the National Railway Museum at York.

The British Austerity locomotives were designed and built to assist the war effort. As the name implies, they were of a simple design capable of being produced quickly in large numbers. The first appeared from Vulcan Foundry in May 1943. Many of these locomotives were to eventually find their way into British Railways stock where they were to become invaluable and well known. Withdrawals commenced in the late fifties with the last 280 examples remaining in service almost to the very end of steam on British Railways. In the final years the twenty-five examples of the 2–10–0 version were all allocated to the Scottish Region, withdrawals of the entire class taking place in 1961/2.

In the late forties, renumbering into the BR series commenced, with nos 90000–90732 being allocated to the 2–8–0s, and nos 90750–90774 to the 2–10–0s. They were also officially known as 8F WD class. For many enthusiasts the nickname 'Dub Dee' will always be how they will be remembered, and despite attempts to lose the term Austerity, this is how they are still widely referred to among many railwaymen and enthusiasts.

Fresh from works overhaul, the WDs looked very smart in unlined black livery. This did not last very long, however, as they soon acquired a coat of grime, since engine cleaning at depots was confined mainly to passenger engines. In the sixties many WDs were to be seen in a deplorable state. As they became due for works overhaul their characteristic clanking sounds became even more pronounced, and at this time they became extremely rough riding.

WDs were a regular daily sight on the East Coast main line, where one of the principal duties of the stud allocated to New England was hauling heavy coal trains to Ferme Park. Although they were very common, I never lost the opportunity of recording them on film. On rare occasions they were to be seen on passenger trains, having taken over at short notice from a failed engine when nothing more suitable was available. Unfortunately, I never saw one, although I can recall a WD heading the New England breakdown train travelling at speed on its way to an incident, and on another occasion a member of the class worked the train to re-rail a J15 class 0–6–0 at Huntingdon East. This involved running through the very tight curved platforms at this station which has long since gone. The squealing flanges which accompanied this movement on lines that never usually saw anything larger than a 2MT 2–6–0 is something I shall long remember.

The last WDs in service were usually in a terrible state, with large accumulations of soot, oil and grease being commonplace and often almost completely obscuring the cabside number. None of the British Railways 2–8–0s or 2–10–0s survived to be rescued for preservation. However, there are some examples still to be seen: these are locomotives that were purchased by other countries after the war and in recent years have also returned home. The North British Locomotive Company built 2–10–0 no. 73651 *Gordon*, formerly used on the Longmoor military railway.

Although I can remember the WD 2–10–0s in action south of the border it was not until the mid-fifties that the opportunity arose for me to record examples on film; by this time they were all to be found at Carlisle or Scottish depots.

This is a volume of contrasts. The Austerities were built with a single purpose in mind, many of them going on to give over twenty years' service. In contrast, the Standard designs were well thought out, offered vast improvements over many earlier locomotives both in efficiency and comfort for the enginemen, but had comparatively limited (and in some cases very short) working lives. Nevertheless, both Standards and Austerities were a very important part of our railway history. Fortunately quite a number have survived, some of which can still be seen in action, although four classes were to become extinct, the final examples falling victim to the scrapman's cutting torch.

Design and Introduction into Service

As early as 1942 the locomotive requirements of the British Army for the future liberation of Europe were being planned. Established classes such as the Great Central 04 2–8–0s and Stanier 8F 2–8–0s had already been rejected, the latter on the grounds of the amount of materials and labour involved in their construction. It was decided to prepare an entirely new basic design, quick and economical to build and easy to maintain, and, once the war was over, expendable.

The result was the Austerity, designed by R.A. Riddles, aided by T.F. Coleman, the chief locomotive draughtsman of the LMS. The first of these 2–8–0s appeared in 1943. Eventually, over a three-year period, 935 were built by the North British Locomotive Company and the Vulcan Foundry. The 2–10–0 version also appeared in 1943; these were basically the same but had a wider firebox and grate area, the lower axle weight resulting in higher route availability. In all, 150 examples of this type were constructed by the North British Locomotive Company.

These War Department engines were to become well known on our railway system before their service abroad commenced in 1944. After the end of hostilities in 1945 locomotives started to return home. The LNER purchased 200 the following year, and following nationalisation in 1948 British Railways bought 533 2–8–0s and 25 2–10–0s. Considering that they were built for comparatively short use they did remarkably well, the last 2–10–0 not being withdrawn until 1962 and the final 2–8–0 being condemned in 1967, only one year before steam ended on British Railways.

With the formation of the state-owned system it was soon established that a range of standard steam locomotives would be required. Main line diesels had already been introduced by the LMS but development of these was such that steam power was expected to continue for many more years. Mr R.A. Riddles was appointed a member of the Railway Executive with responsibility for mechanical and electrical engineering, which involved development of the new locomotive designs. He was assisted by R.C. Bond and E.S. Cox. They needed time to design and plan the new locomotives. Additional locomotives to classes already introduced by the 'Big Four' continued to be constructed well into the British Railways era. It was in 1951 that the first Standard design appeared (the 'Britannia' class), followed by several others later that same year. Considerable changes took place in the intended designs during the early years, but eventually twelve types were built, totalling 999 locomotives. Some were destined to have very short working lives owing to electrification and the large-scale introduction of diesels. A number of tender designs were included in the British Railways Standard classes, and within the Standards locomotives could be found paired with different tender types. This has generally not been detailed in this volume.

We are fortunate that a considerable number of standard locomotives have survived into preservation, although there were four designs where none has survived.

BRITISH RAILWAYS STANDARD CLASSES

The Standard Classes

Class	Numbers	Years	Total Built
7MT 4–6–2 'Britannia'	70000	1951–4	55
8P 4–6–2 'Duke'	71000	1953	1
6MT 4–6–2 'Clans'	72000	1951	10
5MT 4–6–0	73000	1951–57	172
4MT 4–6–0	75000	1951–7	80
4MT 2–6–0	76000	1952–7	115
3MT 2–6–0	77000	1954	20
2MT 2–6–0	78000	1952–6	65
4MT 2–6–4T	80000	1951–6	155
3MT 2–6–2T	82000	1952–5	45
2MT 2–6–2T	84000	1953–7	30
9F 2–10–0	92000	1954–60	251

Locomotive stock in 1960:   999

Quite often the Cambridge–Bletchley trains included one or more horseboxes. No. 80082 is seen here in the south bay at Cambridge, ready with a morning departure. The services were mostly worked by Standard 4MT 4–6–0s of the 75000 series and 4MT 2–6–4Ts at this time.

9.5.55

70000 'Britannia' class 7MT 4–6–2

Introduced: 1951
Total built: 55

Principal dimensions:

Weight:	locomotive	94 tons
	tender	47 or 55 tons (depending on type)
Boiler pressure:		250 lb sq. in
Driving wheels:		6 ft 2 in
Tractive effort:		32,150 lb
Cylinders:		20 in × 28 in
Walschaerts valve gear		

Number series: 70000–70054. All were named with the exception of no. 70047.

70000	*Britannia*		70027	*Rising Star*
70001	*Lord Hurcomb*		70028	*Royal Star*
70002	*Geoffrey Chaucer*		70029	*Shooting Star*
70003	*John Bunyan*		70030	*William Wordsworth*
70004	*William Shakespeare*		70031	*Byron*
70005	*John Milton*		70032	*Tennyson*
70006	*Robert Burns*		70033	*Charles Dickens*
70007	*Coeur-de-Lion*		70034	*Thomas Hardy*
70008	*Black Prince*		70035	*Rudyard Kipling*
70009	*Alfred the Great*		70036	*Boadicea*
70010	*Owen Glendower*		70037	*Hereward the Wake*
70011	*Hotspur*		70038	*Robin Hood*
70012	*John of Gaunt*		70039	*Sir Christopher Wren*
70013	*Oliver Cromwell*		70040	*Clive of India*
70014	*Iron Duke*		70041	*Sir John Moore*
70015	*Apollo*		70042	*Lord Roberts*
70016	*Ariel*		70043	*Lord Kitchener*
70017	*Arrow*		70044	*Earl Haig*
70018	*Flying Dutchman*		70045	*Lord Rowallan*
70019	*Lightning*		70046	*Anzac*
70020	*Mercury*		70048	*The Territorial Army 1908–58*
70021	*Morning Star*		70049	*Solway Firth*
70022	*Tornado*		70050	*Firth of Clyde*
70023	*Venus*		70051	*Firth of Forth*
70024	*Vulcan*		70052	*Firth of Tay*
70025	*Western Star*		70053	*Moray Firth*
70026	*Polar Star*		70054	*Dornoch Firth*

Two survive: no. 70000 *Britannia* and no. 70013 *Oliver Cromwell*

The 'Britannias' were the first of the twelve Standard classes to appear. The first, no. 70000 *Britannia*, was completed at Crewe Works in January 1951. In all fifty-five locomotives were built, all at Crewe. The entire class was named, except no. 70047, but in some cases the names were not carried immediately. *Britannia* itself was named at Marylebone by the then Minister of Transport. No. 70049 *Solway Firth* was the last to receive its name, in May 1960.

These engines naturally created considerable interest at the time: 1951 was the year of the Festival of Britain, and what better place to put one of these brand new locomotives on public display. No. 70004 *William Shakespeare* was given special treatment at Crewe Works and dispatched to the South Bank site in London. On arrival it was given a final polish before the exhibition opened.

The first batch of these locomotives was allocated to Norwich and Stratford depots to work expresses, at that time in the hands of 'Sandringhams' and B1 class 4–6–0s. The 'Britannias' were to make a vast difference even on the new fast schedules introduced shortly after their arrival. As more locomotives became available, examples of the class started to appear regularly at Cambridge. Two 'Britannias', nos 70004 *William Shakespeare* and 70014 *Iron Duke*, were allocated to Stewarts Lane depot: among their duties was the 'Golden Arrow' service. Locomotives of the class were also sent to the Western Region with Old Oak Common and Laira (Plymouth) depots each having several, and a solitary example at Newton Abbot. 'Britannias' were to be seen on services to Bristol, South Wales and Penzance, with the London Midland and Scottish regions also receiving examples. The British Railways Standard classes were designed to have a route availability as wide as was permitted within weight restrictions; this policy resulted in these locomotives being found on all regions at some time during their working life.

As with the Standard class 5s, two 'Britannias', nos 70043 *Lord Kitchener* and 70044 *Earl Haig*, were fitted with Westinghouse pumps in 1953 for experimental work on high-speed air-braked freights. By the early sixties diesel locomotives were taking over many of the steam turns. The days of 'Britannias' on the Great Eastern Liverpool Street services were over, and the 'Britannias' were transferred to March depot, a shed principally concerned with goods traffic. With such an influx of engines some were soon to be seen stored in the yard.

In late 1960 a number of 'Britannias' were transferred to Immingham depot. This shed was responsible for the Cleethorpes–Kings Cross service, which it worked with immaculate B1 class 4–6–0s, as well as a number of fast fish trains. In due course the 'Britannias' replaced the B1s on this service which then provided the only regular workings of these engines on passenger services on the East Coast main line south of Peterborough. The train had a fast schedule on the Kings Cross–Peterborough section, running non-stop on the Up service and stopping at Huntingdon in the early evening on the return. 'Britannias' could be seen taking the long 1 in 200 climb to Abbots Ripton with the twelve-coach train with ease from a standing start at Huntingdon. In 1963 diesels replaced the 'Britannias', bringing this service to an end. Meanwhile, the engines at March were about to move to the London Midland Region. By this time some which had been stored for a period of time were in poor external condition, with a considerable number based in the Carlisle area.

Only one locomotive, no. 70013 *Oliver Cromwell* survived into 1968, the others being withdrawn at the end of 1967. No. 70013 was transferred to Carnforth, where, in the few remaining months of steam on British Railways, it was much in demand for use on enthusiasts specials. On the final day of steam working no. 70013 was in action from Liverpool to Carlisle via the Settle & Carlisle. I well recall seeing the engine on this route:

thousands of people had turned out to watch it passing, and the traffic congestion on the narrow roads was almost unbelievable. *Oliver Cromwell* was destined for preservation at Bressingham, and made its final run under its own power to Norwich, from where it was towed to Diss, making the remainder of the journey by road. For a considerable period the engine was regularly in steam at the Museum, but for some years now it has been on display as a static exhibit.

The other survivor of the class is no. 70000 *Britannia*. For years this engine worked on the Great Eastern section until it was displaced and transferred to March. Much to my surprise in September 1961 this engine appeared at Huntingdon hauling a northbound fast goods on what was normally a V2 duty. *Britannia* was still allocated to March at this time, and engines from this depot were unusual south of Peterborough. In March 1963 no. 70000 was allocated to Willesden, later moving to Crewe North and then Crewe South before moving to its final shed, Newton Heath, in March 1966. It was withdrawn from here just two months later. It was scheduled for preservation as part of the National Collection and was sent initially to Stratford Works for storage, later transferring to Preston Park. While there it suffered damage to the extent that no. 70013 *Oliver Cromwell* was substituted. Fortunately *Britannia* was purchased privately and has survived, working at many different locations over the years.

My first opportunity to photograph one of the new 'Britannias' was of no. 70017 *Arrow* at Old Oak Common depot, London, when the engine was just three months old. One of the first to be allocated to the Western Region, it was fitted with a handrail on the smoke deflectors; these were removed in later days. *Arrow* was later transferred to the London Midland Region, ending its days at Carlisle Kingmoor, in September 1966.

9.9.51

Every so often in steam days the opportunity arose of photographing a rare engine or working. This is one such. Expecting the usual V2 or A3 on the afternoon fast goods from Kings Cross, I was very surprised when no. 70000 *Britannia* turned up. At this time it was a March engine, and how it came to be on this working I never found out. Locomotives from March were very rare south of Peterborough. Examples of this class were only seen on the East Coast main line on the Kings Cross–Cleethorpes service, and then only for a short time before diesels took over. There were, of course, examples of the class working on enthusiasts specials on this section.

9.61

March acquired a number of 'Britannias' in 1960/1 which were mostly used on freight workings. No. 70001 *Lord Hurcomb* was photographed awaiting its next duty. Steam was already running down at the depot which was a shadow of its former self, with a number of engines stored in the yard. This engine was to be allocated to two more depots, Willesden and Aston, before ending up at Carlisle Kingmoor, from where it was withdrawn in September 1966, ending its days at the Motherwell Machinery & Scrap Co., Wishaw, in early 1967.

9.9.62

It seemed that whenever I visited Stratford shed it was a gloomy grey day with a smoky atmosphere. It was a fascinating place in the mid-fifties with over 400 engines allocated, including 13 'Britannias'. No. 70011 *Hotspur* was a Norwich engine, pictured here awaiting its return working. Note the headcode, one disc and one lamp.

7.5.55

It was not long before Norwich depot 'Britannias' were to be seen at Cambridge, especially as more became available for the East Anglian services. This is no. 70012 *John of Gaunt*, photographed on Cambridge shed. These locomotives soon became popular with enginemen who had spent years on 'Clauds' and 'Sandringhams', the latter often being rough riding, especially when due a general overhaul.

2.8.52

Time for a smoke as no. 70002 *Geoffrey Chaucer* takes water at Cambridge. Note the massive column of the water crane; this one was used extensively in steam days. The impressive signal gantry was a feature of the north end of Cambridge, and for many years controlled the long main platform and two bays to the left of this picture.

10.8.55

No. 70007 *Coeur-de-Lion* at March shed. At this time fully fitted freights to York were among the duties allocated to the 'Britannias'. This engine was transferred to Carlisle Kingmoor in December 1963, having the distinction of being the first of the class to be withdrawn. It was condemned in June 1965. After a short period in store at Crewe it was cut up there in July 1965.

14.7.63

During the fifties 'Britannias' could be seen on the West Coast main line. No. 70031 *Byron* drifts into Rugby at the head of a thirteen-coach Manchester–Euston train. This locomotive was allocated to Longsight (Manchester) shed at the time and it was to remain there for several years, ending its days at Carlisle, from where it was withdrawn in November 1967.

29.5.54

Another picture of no. 70001 *Lord Hurcomb* at March. One of the initial batch allocated to the Great Eastern section, it was completed at Crewe in February 1951 and sent to Stratford depot. Naming took place at Liverpool Street station on 6 February 1951. The engine remained at Stratford until February 1959 when it went to Norwich, moving on to March two years later when diesels had taken over the London–Norwich services. *Lord Hurcomb* also had a short period in store at March before moving to the London Midland Region.

9.9.62

When the Britannias were transferred to March shed after being displaced by diesels at Stratford and Norwich depots, there was not enough work for all the engines. Several were placed in store, having been greased down and their chimneys covered with a piece of tarpaulin. No. 70003 *John Bunyan* still had a fully coaled tender. This particular engine was stored for three months before being transferred to Carlisle Kingmoor from where it was withdrawn in March 1967.

9.63

In mid-1963 March depot had in store a number of engines of several classes. No. 70030 *William Wordsworth* keeps company with an 01 class 2–8–0. Originally a London Midland Region engine first allocated to Holyhead, *William Wordsworth* was not transferred to the Eastern Region until 1954, initially on loan. Along with its classmates, it was then transferred to the London Midland Region, being withdrawn in June 1966 and cut up at Wards of Beighton, Sheffield.

23.6.63

No. 70020 *Mercury*, photographed at its home depot, Old Oak Common. The engine has obviously run into problems, as part of the footplating, buffer beam and buffer have been removed. Along with others on the Western Region, the Old Oak Common 'Britannias' were transferred to Cardiff (Canton), where the footplate crews soon became very familiar with these engines. This helped to eliminate problems that could arise where enginemen only worked on them occasionally.

7.8.55

No. 70020 *Mercury*, photographed at Peterborough in October 1964, when it was allocated to 1A Willesden, having spent time at several other sheds since leaving the Western Region in October 1961. The locomotive was working the Home Counties Railway Society Special to York. 'Britannias' were often seen on enthusiasts specials in the final years of steam.

4.10.64

The Standard designs were built to give a wide range of availability. No. 70054 *Dornoch Firth* was the last of the class to be built, being completed in October 1954 and going to Polmadie (Glasgow) where this picture was taken. This engine was to spend a year at Banbury before going to its final shed, Carlisle Kingmoor, from where it was withdrawn in November 1966, later going north of the border to a scrapyard at Wishaw.

26.8.55

Time was rapidly running out for no. 70010 *Owen Glendower*, photographed here at Crewe South shed. It was then a Carlisle engine, having just seven months' service left. The original nameplates had been removed, and the name at this time was painted on, although many examples of the class did not even have this. 'Britannias' in early 1967 were mostly to be seen on fitted goods, parcels and the occasional passenger train.

12.2.67

Leeds Holbeck depot, 1966. No. 70016 *Ariel*, minus nameplates and in a run-down condition, is seen in company with two 'Peak' diesels. *Ariel* would almost certainly have worked to Leeds over the Settle & Carlisle route. At this time many of the 'Britannias' were to be found at Carlisle. Two were withdrawn in 1965, with many more following in 1966, and massive inroads being made in 1967. Happily, two examples have survived into preservation.

20.3.66

'Britannias' were only to be seen on the East Coast main line south of Peterborough for two years, during which time they were well maintained by Immingham depot and used on the Kings Cross service. No. 70040 *Clive of India* starts the long 1 in 200 climb from Huntingdon in brilliant early evening sunshine. In December 1963 the Immingham engines were sent to Carlisle, having been replaced by diesels.

9.61

'Britannias' were still seen on passenger services in 1964. This is no. 70008 *Black Prince* at Beattock with a lightly loaded semi-fast to Glasgow. Steam is leaking freely from the right-hand cylinder, but whether it completed the journey or failed en route is not known. It remained in service at Carlisle until January 1967.

18.9.64

This locomotive was one of the final batch, going new to Polmadie. No. 70052 *Firth of Tay*, minus nameplates, was allocated to Banbury when this picture was taken. It only remained at this shed for a year before being transferred to Carlisle from where it was withdrawn in November 1966. In their final years many 'Britannias' lost their nameplates. As can be seen, the engine was in a deplorable condition by this time.

27.10.65

Crewe South shed on a gloomy October day and no. 70024 *Vulcan*, minus nameplates, has just run off the turntable. It had been a Crewe engine just before this picture being taken but was then transferred to Carlisle. The engine carries no shedplate; many others did not do so at this time, although the shed number was usually stencilled or painted on. It remained in service until December 1967 before being sent to Wards of Killamarsh for scrap.

16.10.66

One of the two surviving 'Britannias' is no. 70013 *Oliver Cromwell*, which had the distinction of hauling the farewell steam special in August 1968, after which it went to Bressingham where it has remained ever since. In the early years it was frequently in steam, as on this occasion at a special February opening, just a few months after its arrival. Note that the name is painted on and it has acquired a Norwich shedplate. This locomotive is part of the National Collection.

2.2.69

71000 *Duke of Gloucester* 8P 4–6–2

Introduced: 1954
Total built: 1

Principal dimensions:

Weight:	locomotive	101 tons 5 cwt
	tender	55 tons 10 cwt
Boiler pressure:		250 lb sq. in
Driving wheels:		6 ft 2 in
Tractive effort:		39,080 lb
Cylinders (3):		18 in × 28 in

British Caprotti valve gear (outside)

Only one was built, no. 71000 *Duke of Gloucester*, which has survived into preservation.

In the planning stage for the Standard designs provision was made for a new large express passenger design, initially based on the very successful Stanier 'Duchess' class with four cylinders, bar frames, double blastpipe and chimney. The motive power situation during the early fifties, with no immediate requirement for locomotives of this type, resulted in little design work being done. However, as a result of the Harrow & Wealdstone crash, no. 46202 *Princess Anne*, which had only recently been rebuilt from the experimental 'Turbomotive', had to be withdrawn. As the London Midland Region was now short of one Pacific, no. 71000 *Duke of Gloucester* was the subject of special authorisation. The original large Pacific plans were abandoned, and the locomotive was a BR Standard, three-cylinder, express passenger locomotive, fitted with British Caprotti valve gear, double chimney and blastpipe. It was the last new Pacific design for British Railways and emerged from Crewe Works in 1954. Although it was not envisaged at the time of production, it was to have a comparatively short working life of just eight years, mainly because of the introduction of diesel and electric traction.

Although it was very economical in terms of steam consumption, there were some problems, principally concerning boiler performance and efficiency at high power outputs. This powerful locomotive gained a reputation for being heavy on coal, placing great demands on the fireman when it was working on full power. For much of its life the engine was allocated to Crewe North shed.

Locomotive crews accustomed to Stanier Pacifics found this engine very different. With enthusiastic enginemen the *Duke* performed well, and was often to be seen on the 'Midday Scot'. Had this engine been built earlier then doubtless the problems would have been resolved. But it was a time of change, the decision having already been made to stop steam locomotive building and to change to diesel and electric traction. In November 1962 no. 71000 was withdrawn in full working order, having clocked up some 280,000 miles in its eight years' service.

Then followed a series of events which finally resulted in the engine ending up at the famous Woodham Bros scrapyard at Barry; had this not happened it would certainly not be with us today. Originally the *Duke of Gloucester* had been listed for preservation as part of the National Collection, and in view of this was placed in store. A change to the original plans resulted in this being cancelled, with just the left-hand cylinder and valve gear being removed, sectioned and put on display at the Science Museum. When this work was done, with both cylinders having been removed (presumably to balance the engine), the sad remains stood in Crewe Works yard minus chimney, smoke deflectors and other parts. In due course the mutilated locomotive was sold to Woodhams, where its fate was nearly sealed. However, it was in fact delivered to Cashmores of Newport, where, had it not been for someone noting the label reading 'Woodhams, Barry' it would have been cut up. Fortunately, the locomotive was towed to its rightful destination. Then followed seven years of exposure to salt-laden air and all that the weather could throw at it. As time went by corrosion and the efforts of souvenir hunters among the many visitors who made their way to Barry resulted in the remains becoming even more derelict. The locomotive tender had been taken to a steelworks where the chassis was used in the transportation of steel. Locomotives which had stood at Barry for years were being purchased and taken away in increasing numbers. On 24 April 1974 it was the *Duke's* turn. It left Barry looking very different, having received a cosmetic coat of paint and fitted with a double chimney and smoke deflectors from a 9F, and moved to its new home, the Great Central Railway, Loughborough.

Then began the seemingly impossible task of restoration to full working order. It was a mammoth undertaking. But such was the determination of the team involved that even major problems such as the replacement of the two outside cylinders and Caprotti poppet valve gear were overcome. Eventually, after a magnificent effort by all involved, the locomotive was completed in October 1985, passing its static steam test with flying colours. The locomotive was completed for working by the following year and since then the *Duke of Gloucester* has worked a great many trains, in the process becoming one of the most popular of the preserved Pacifics.

Anyone looking at the mutilated no. 71000 *Duke of Gloucester* in Crewe Works yard in 1966 could not possibly have thought that this locomotive would ever run again. Both cylinders had been removed, together with the windshields and chimney, valve gear and coupling rods. Originally intended for preservation, this decision was for some reason later reversed, with only the left-hand cylinder and valve gear to be saved.

16.10.66

72000 'Clan' class 6MT 4–6–2

Introduced: 1951
Total built: 10

Principal dimensions:

Weight:	locomotive	86 tons 19 cwt
	tender	47 tons 2 cwt
Boiler pressure:		225 lb sq. in
Driving wheels:		6 ft 2 in
Tractive effort:		27,520 lb
Cylinders:		19.5 in × 28 in
Walschaerts valve gear		

Number series: 72000–72009. All ten locomotives were named.

72000	*Clan Buchanan*		72005	*Clan MacGregor*
72001	*Clan Cameron*		72006	*Clan MacKenzie*
72002	*Clan Campbell*		72007	*Clan MacIntosh*
72003	*Clan Fraser*		72008	*Clan MacLeod*
72004	*Clan MacDonald*		72009	*Clan Stewart*

Another Standard locomotive class to make its debut in 1951 was the 'Clans'. These had smaller boiler and cylinders than the 'Britannias' but otherwise had many similarities, with identical chassis, driving wheel size and wheel spacing. The 'Clans', with their 6MT rating, never quite matched up to expectations and the many class 5 4–6–0s were capable of handling most trains. As a result only ten 'Clans' were built, although it had been originally intended to construct more, preference being given to the more powerful 'Britannias'.

The 'Clans' were built at Crewe Works in 1951/2. The first five were allocated to Polmadie and the others to Carlisle Kingmoor. There was a certain amount of movement, mostly to Scottish Region depots, and some returning to Kingmoor. One, no. 72009 *Clan Stewart*, was transferred to Stratford, London, for a month in 1958 for trials, but as Stratford and other East Anglian depots were already well served by 'Britannias', it soon returned to Kingmoor. There were many occasions when examples worked south, but by and large they were to be found in Scotland or the Carlisle area. Engines from this depot included duties on the Settle & Carlisle line, and for a time the 'Clans' worked the 'Waverley'. Other duties were on the West Coast main line, including the Glasgow–Liverpool and Manchester trains, parcels and fast goods. In their final years 'Clans' were to be found on enthusiasts specials, often taking them to unfamiliar territory.

In December 1962 the Scottish Region withdrew all five locomotives under its control, after which they were stored first at Polmadie and later at Parkhead. In October 1963 they made their final move, this time to Darlington Works. Here they were stored for a short period, before the first was scrapped in February 1964. The remaining five engines were at Carlisle Kingmoor which had become a London Midland Region depot in

February 1958; this in effect gave them a further lease of life and it was not until May 1965 that no. 72005 was condemned, and the last to go was no. 72006 in May 1966. All were cut up at private scrapyards in Scotland, and none has survived into preservation.

The class was not particularly popular with enginemen, although this did vary between depots to some extent. They gained the reputation of being poor steamers, but the Carlisle enginemen found that if driven hard they could perform well with heavy loads even on the difficult West Coast main line.

Although I saw members of the 'Clan' class in operation, I was never in the right place at the right time to record one on film. These locomotives spent their working lives based at Scottish depots and Carlisle Kingmoor, and they did not work south of the border. No. 72007 *Clan MacKintosh* was a Kingmoor engine throughout its working life, but it is seen here at Polmadie. Five of the class had already been withdrawn. No. 72007 followed in December 1965 and was cut up at Campbells scrapyard, Airdrie, in March 1996. The last example was condemned in May 1966.

Photograph: Alan Blencowe

73000 class 5MT 4–6–0

Introduced: 1951
Total built: 172

Principal dimensions:

Weight:	locomotive	76 tons
	tender	47 tons 4 cwt (plus variations)
Boiler pressure:		225 lb
Driving wheels:		6 ft 2 in
Tractive effort:		26,120 lb
Cylinders:		19 in × 28 in

Walschaerts valve gear
British Caprotti (outside): nos 73125–73154

Number series: 73000–73171. None carried names in early BR days but the Southern Region later named twenty, giving them former 'King Arthur' class names, and all were fitted with new cast nameplates.

73080	*Merlin*	73110	*The Red Knight*
73081	*Excalibur*	73111	*King Uther*
73082	*Camelot*	73112	*Morgan Le Fay*
73083	*Pendragon*	73113	*Lyonesse*
73084	*Tintagel*	73114	*Etarre*
73085	*Melisande*	73115	*King Pellinore*
73086	*The Green Knight*	73116	*Iseult*
73087	*Linette*	73117	*Vivien*
73088	*Joyous Gard*	73118	*King Leodegrance*
73089	*Maid of Astolat*	73119	*Elaine*

Five members of the class are in preservation, one of which, no. 73129, is a Caprotti engine.

In 1951 great interest was aroused in railway circles by the appearance of several British Railways Standard classes, among them the class 5MT 4–6–0s. The first of these, no. 73000, was put on display at Marylebone on 26 April 1951, fresh from Derby Works. Eventually, 172 engines of this class would be built between 1951 and 1957, the vast majority at Derby and the remainder at Doncaster, and a number of different tender types were fitted to these engines. Thirty, nos 73125–73154, were fitted with British Caprotti valve gear, and all of these were built at Derby in 1956/7. When new the first ten went to Shrewsbury, after two years moving to Patricroft, which was to become the home shed for the majority of the 'Caprotti 5s', the exceptions being nos 73145–54, which were allocated to Scottish Region depots.

The Standard class 5s soon proved themselves and were well liked by the enginemen. The 'Caprottis' were widely regarded as good strong locomotives capable of handling all types of work. Two members of the class, nos 73030/1, built at Derby in 1952, were fitted with Westinghouse brakes for fitted freight train trials. (Similar trials were carried out on two 'Britannia' class locomotives.)

Batches of these fine engines were built for all regions. A considerable number went to the Scottish Region where they worked on the Highland line and Glasgow to Aberdeen, often on named trains. They were, of course, a familiar sight in many other parts of Scotland. Only a small number were allocated to the Eastern Region, and most of these were to be found on the Great Central. Two examples were to spend a short time at Kings Cross, no. 73071 in 1956 and no. 73159 in 1957. During their stay they worked local services to Cambridge and Peterborough and on occasions were used on special trains.

None of the class was named when built, but the Southern Region subsequently allocated names to twenty examples, nos 73080–73089 and 73110–73119. These names were carried on new plates fixed on the side of the footplating. Several of these engines were to be seen in their final years working local services into Waterloo and also on carriage pilot duties at Clapham Junction. One of them, no. 73082 *Camelot*, withdrawn from Guildford in June 1966, still survives in preservation, as do four others including Caprotti no. 73129 which ended its days at Patricroft in December 1967. In their final years the class 5s were often seen in a deplorable condition, in many cases minus the front number plate. Several of those that survived into the final year of steam working on British Railways were often seen on enthusiasts specials in good external condition. The pioneer engine, no. 73000, allocated to Patricroft until March 1968, has not survived, having been cut up at Cashmores scrapyard, Great Bridge. Only one of the engines still working in 1968 has survived, no. 73050, now named *City of Peterborough*.

Two standard class 5s were built with Westinghouse brake equipment for working fitted freight train trials. No. 73031 was the second of these engines; it is seen here brand new at Derby while undergoing running-in trials; it later spent some time at Rugby testing station. The compressor can be seen mounted on the side of the smokebox and the reservoir below the running plate in front of the cab. The special equipment was later removed from both engines. After extensive trials no. 73031 ended its days at Oxford from where it was withdrawn in September 1965 and cut up at Cashmores, Newport.

10.7.53

The majority of the Standard class 5s were built at Derby. Here, brand new no. 73032 stands in the shed yard undergoing steaming trials; note the red flag on the buffer beam, indicating the engine is not to be moved. Construction of these engines continued for seven years, the last batch being built at Doncaster.

10.7.53

During the fifties Standard 5s were to be found over a very wide area. No. 73060 is seen here at Polmadie, a shed I will always remember for its lighting poles, five of which can be seen in this picture. No. 73060 was one of a batch of these engines allocated to Polmadie, from where it was withdrawn in May 1967, ending its days at Campbells, Airdrie, just five months later.

26.8.55

This is no. 73071 on strange territory at Cambridge depot, where it was to remain for several weeks awaiting the arrival of new rocking grate. No. 73071 and a Stanier class 5 no. 44911 were transferred from Chester to Kings Cross depot for a year for automatic train control equipment trials. Within a short time no. 73071 was in trouble, hence its stay at Cambridge. These engines were not usually seen here at the time although one is thought to have worked in via March previously.

26.2.56

For most of its time at Kings Cross, no. 73071 worked the Cambridge service. Here the engine is seen leaving Hitchin on its way to London. On other occasions it worked semi-fasts to Peterborough, but owing to an engine failure in an Immingham depot B1 4–6–0, it also worked the Kings Cross–Cleethorpes service. After a year no. 73071 and no. 44911 returned to Chester.

14.10.56

Running on clear signals no. 73099 speeds through Bletchley at the head of a Stephenson Locomotive Society special, comprising mostly Eastern Region stock. The Cambridge line can be seen to the far right of the picture. No. 73099 ended its days at Polmadie, being condemned in October 1966. Note the tall signal with its repeater arms.

29.4.56

Bristol had three major locomotive depots, two for the Western Region and the third, the Barrow Road shed, code 22a, for the London Midland Region. No. 73028, seen here at the latter, was actually one of the seven Standard class 5s allocated to Bristol St Phillips Marsh. This engine spent several years in the area before going to Swindon, Gloucester, Oxley and finally Bolton where the end came in December 1966.

31.8.55

During the mid-fifties the Somerset & Dorset offered a fascinating range of motive power, and the S & D 2–8–0s were still active. Veteran 0–6–0s were still to be seen on local goods duties, while modern motive power in the form of Standard class 5s was allocated to Bath depot. One of these was no. 73049, seen here at its home shed.

31.8.55

No. 73052, one of the batch allocated to the Bath depot, stands alongside 3F no. 43201, a true Somerset & Dorset veteran built for the S & DJ line and taken into LMS stock in 1930. The Standard class 5 ended its days at this shed, being condemned in December 1964. It was one of fourteen withdrawn that year when inroads were first made into the class. No. 73052 was cut up at Buttigiegs scrapyard, Newport, in April 1965.

31.8.55

Thirty Standard class 5 were built with Caprotti valve gear at Derby Works in 1956–7 and these engines proved to be very powerful. In the sixties they were often to be seen at Llandudno Junction depot where this picture of no. 73135 was taken. At the time it was allocated to Patricroft, where those examples of this type south of the border were concentrated in the final years, and along with numerous others of its class, it was cut up at Cashmores scrapyard, Great Bridge.

12.6.66

This picture illustrates clearly the Caprotti valve gear on no. 73144. To maintain these engines in good working order required a degree of specialised knowledge. Only in their final years were they concentrated at one English depot, Patricroft, with a small number north of the border.

12.7.64

Ten of the Caprotti valve engines, nos 73135–73144, were fitted with the type BR1C flush-sided tender with a capacity of 9 tons of coal and 4,725 gallons of water. No. 73144, photographed at Llandudno Junction, was the last of this batch. These engines and the Caprotti 'Black Fives' were regularly seen on the North Wales line.

12.6.64

This close-up view shows the Caprotti rotary cam poppet valve gear on Standard class 5 no. 73135. The major advantage of this system was its excellent steam distribution. All staff, especially the enginemen, had to be familiar with the operation of these engines in order to obtain the best results.

12.6.66

Even on a Sunday in the mid-sixties Llandudno Junction depot still had a considerable number of engines on shed, many of them Stanier 'Black Fives'. Examples of the Standard version, including Caprottis, which had worked in from Manchester, were usually also to be found. No. 73135 was one of these. In the background is class 5 no. 45004 and to the right a 'Jinty' 3F 0–6–0T.

12.6.66

Typical of the condition of many steam locomotives in their final years, this is no. 73158. The smokebox number and shedplate have gone, the locomotive number has been chalked on but is barely visible, while the cabside number is obscured by layers of grime. At this time, no. 73158 was allocated to Bedford for a few weeks before going back to Cricklewood and finally Patricroft.

30.6.63

Engines from South Wales depots were often to be found at Oxford and Banbury depots. This is no. 73025 of Cardiff Canton, photographed in a grimy condition at Banbury. During its working life this engine appeared in the allocation of several depots, finally going to Patricroft and ending its working life in October 1967. It was towed to Cashmores of Newport for scrapping.

27.3.55

Often, on visits to locomotive depots, engine shunting movements have enabled me to take a picture that would otherwise be impossible, often during the few minutes before the engine concerned disappeared back into the depths of the shed. No. 73070 was engaged on this type of work at Shrewsbury when I took this picture. It was fitted with a type BR1C flush-sided tender.

21.7.64

Pictured at Exeter shed, this is no. 73028 of Bristol St Phillips Marsh, already prepared for its return working. This was the only Standard engine present, all the others being Great Western types. In the background are two old coaches long since relegated to departmental duties. These were commonplace in the fifties but very few enthusiasts took the opportunity to record them on film.

4.9.56

The cold foggy conditions did little to improve this picture of a run-down, grubby Standard class 5 no. 73068 at Bath Green Park station, with steam leaking from several points. Time was running out for this engine and just two months later it was withdrawn from service. The front number plate had already gone, replaced by a crudely painted number.

26.10.65

No. 73020 runs into Brockenhurst station with a semi-fast passenger train. At the time it was allocated to Weymouth shed, from where it was moved in April 1967, going to Guildford where it remained until steam finished on the Southern Region in July of that year. No. 73020 was one the many engines sold to and cut up by Cashmores of Newport, South Wales.

16.9.66

The high running plate of these engines can be clearly seen in this picture of no. 73095 at Oswestry depot. The locomotive was allocated to Croes Newydd at the time, later moving to Agecroft where it was to remain for its last four months in service; it was one of the large number of this class withdrawn in 1966.

11.9.65

The Southern Region named twenty of the Standard class 5s using names formerly carried by 'King Arthur' class engines. The new nameplates were carried on the side of the running plate. No. 73088, seen here at Clapham Junction on empty stock duties, was named *Joyous Gard*, but there is no sign of a nameplate. Many of the last steam locomotives working on the Southern ended up at Cashmores of Newport, including this one.

3.3.66

No. 73112 *Morgan Le Fay* runs under the distinctive signal box at Clapham Junction with an empty stock train from Waterloo. Standard 5s were a common sight on these duties at this time. This engine ended its days at Nine Elms in June 1965.

9.61

Another picture of *Morgan Le Fay* at Clapham Junction, clearly showing the nameplate on the running plate between the first two pairs of driving wheels. This picture also illustrates clearly the type BR1F high-sided tender with a capacity of 7 tons of coal and 5,625 gallons of water.

9.61

Standard 5 no. 73111 *King Uther* pulls out of Clapham sidings with an empty stock train under the eagle eye of a 'look-out man' because platelayers are at work on the adjacent track. This engine was transferred to Eastleigh for its final two years of service, being withdrawn in October 1965.

9.61

This is no. 73112 *Morgan Le Fay*, waiting for the signal to proceed. The bottom part of the smokebox door has been repainted. It has no shedplate, but both the front number and the nameplates are intact. Several of these engines were busy on stock workings on this occasion. In due course many of these duties were handed over to Standard 2–6–4Ts.

9.61

Standard class 5s were also used on local services from Basingstoke. No. 73115 *King Pellinore* is seen here at Clapham Junction with a three-coach train. Platelayers can be seen near the front of the engine, watching as it crosses the section of track they were working on. No. 73115 was withdrawn from Guildford in March 1967.

9.61

This locomotive, no. 73069, was the last of the class to be withdrawn. In its final years it was allocated to Bolton, Patricroft and Carnforth, the latter for one month only. On several occasions it was used on enthusiasts specials when it looked very different from its appearance here at Banbury. It remained in service until the end of steam on British Railways, ending its days at Cashmores scrapyard, Newport, in March 1969.

27.10.65

This photograph gives some idea of the grime that accumulated on neglected engines; the cabside number is virtually obscured, only the last two digits being clearly visible because someone has cleaned it. No. 73085 was fitted with the type BR1B flush-sided tender having a 7 ton coal capacity. This picture was taken at Weymouth depot, where, apart from Bullied Pacifics, nearly all the other locomotives present were Standard designs.

15.9.66

No. 73040 is pictured here at Bolton, its home shed, in a clean condition having been used on a rail enthusiasts special. This engine was coupled to a type BR1 inset-design tender carrying 4,250 gallons of water and 7 tons of coal. No. 73040 did not quite make it to the end of steam, being withdrawn four months prior to this from Patricroft, ending its days at Cashmores, Great Bridge, in July 1968.

17.3.68

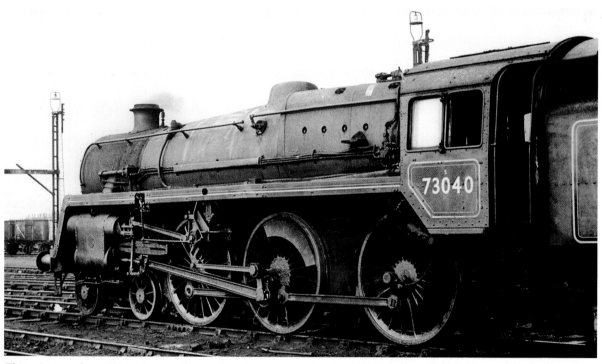

This picture of no. 73040 shows off the clean lines of the Standard 5MT design. In all 172 were built; they were popular with enginemen, powerful and capable of a fair turn of speed. Five have survived into preservation; no. 73096 passed its main line acceptance trials for working enthusiasts specials, the first of which took place in February 1998.

17.3.68

Its working days over, no. 73115 *King Pellinore* has already been prepared for its final journey. The nameplate, smokebox and shed plate have been removed. The valve gear partly dismantled and coupling rods removed, it was towed to Cashmores of Newport and scrapped in November 1967. Withdrawn locomotives travelling in two and threes en route to private scrapyards were a common sight in 1966/7, some of them having stood out of use for months.

4.6.67

At the time of my visit there were more withdrawn engines at Weymouth shed than were still in service. No. 73085 was in a deplorable condition having just used the turntable. Showing up clearly against the dirt and grime are the two white discs over the buffer beam.

15.9.66

75000 class 4MT 4–6–0

Introduced: 1951
Total built: 80

Principal dimensions:

Weight:	locomotive	69 tons
	tender	43 tons 3 cwt
Boiler pressure:		225 lb sq. in
Driving wheels:		5 ft 8 in
Tractive effort:		25,100 lb
Cylinders:		18 in × 28 in
Walschaerts valve gear		

Number series: 75000–75079

Six locomotives of this class survive, including the last two built, nos 75078/9, both constructed at Swindon.

The 75000 series of 4MT lightweight 4–6–0s was another class to make its appearance in 1951. These engines had a wide route availability owing to their low axle loading, and they soon took over from many older designs on a range of duties including working secondary lines. In addition, the fact that they were tender engines meant they had a much greater working range than tank designs. All eighty members of the class were built at Swindon between 1951 and 1957. It had been intended to build a further batch but this was cancelled. When new these engines were fitted with single chimneys, but some of those operating on the Western Region, and all of those on the Southern, were fitted with double blastpipes and chimneys, which not only considerably altered their appearance but more importantly, also improved the performance on what had already proved itself to be a versatile and capable design. The chimney produced for the Western engines was large, rather spoiling the appearance, and was very different from the much neater Eastleigh design. While these engines displaced many older types, within a comparatively short period they were to suffer a similar fate, as diesel locomotives and multiple units replaced them on many lines.

One route on which these very useful engines excelled was the Cambrian; they were to be the last steam locomotives to be used on this line. One of them, no. 75020, was later to be allocated to several sheds before ending up at Carnforth where it was among the last examples in service. It was withdrawn in 1968, ending its days at Campbells of Airdrie.

The class 4s are represented in preservation by six examples. One of these is no. 75014, built at Swindon in 1951. Withdrawn from Shrewsbury in December 1966, it ended up at Woodhams Yard from where it was eventually rescued in February 1981, moving to its new home, the North Yorkshire Moors Railway. Restoration saw this engine in action again during the nineties, not just on its home railway but also performing summer services in Scotland.

Several members of the 75000 class 4MT 4–6–0s have survived into preservation. One of the best known is no. 75014 of the North Yorkshire Moors Railway, not just on this line but also working elsewhere, especially in Scotland. This picture was taken at Chester as the engine awaited departure for Crewe. Its last shed was Shrewsbury, from where it was withdrawn in December 1966. It was sold to Woodhams of Barry, and after many years here exposed to the salt-laden atmosphere it left for its new home in February 1981.

12.8.52

These lightweight 4–6–0s were ideally suited to the Bletchley–Cambridge line. No. 75034 arrives at Sandy on its return journey via Bedford St John's. The East Coast main line is to the right of the picture. After leaving Sandy the Bletchley line climbed and crossed over the main line; it also carried a considerable amount of freight traffic in the fifties with 8F 2–8–0s and occasionally LNW 0–8–0s to be seen at Sandy on these workings.

31.7.54

Ten of these Standard class 4 4–6–0s were allocated to Bletchley in the mid-fifties, working to London, Cambridge and elsewhere. No. 75037 is seen here in the restricted shed area. The depot was adjacent to the north end of the Down line station platform. No. 75037 ended its days on banking duties at Tebay shed from where it was withdrawn in December 1967.

5.9.54

Standard class 4s were to be found on the Leicester–Peterborough services in the early sixties. Here, no. 75040 of Leicester depot runs alongside the East Coast main line at Walton. The train, four coaches of mixed parentage, was typical of many cross-country services at this time. No. 75040 had many depots over the years, ending up at Carnforth where it was condemned in October 1967.

6.9.62

The Bletchley stud of Standard 4s were mostly used on passenger services. This is no. 75031, seen here leaving the shed yard. The tender fitted is the BR2A type which was also coupled to locomotives of the 76000 and 77000 series. Ready for work with this type of tender, the 75 series engines weighed 110 tons 1 cwt. No. 75031 was one of a batch for the London Midland Region constructed at Swindon in 1953/4.

5.9.54

The various Standard designs were constructed to offer as wide a route availability as possible. In the case of the 75000 series engines especially, this meant that they were frequently moved between depots, as was the case with no. 75032 seen here at Llandudno Junction shed still carrying a special train reporting number at the top of the smokebox. After this picture was taken in 1962 the engine went to five other sheds including Tebay, where it would have been used on banking before going to Carnforth from where it was withdrawn in February 1968.

24.6.62

By the early sixties very few Great Western engines were working on the Cambrian line, having been replaced by four classes of Standards, including the 4MT 4–6–0s. No. 75020, widely seen on passenger services at this time, was in green livery and fitted with a double chimney which gave the class a very different appearance. Here, no. 75020 stands ready to leave Portmadoc with a Pwlhelli train.

25.6.62

This picture of no 75020 has been chosen as it clearly shows the cylinder valve gear and coupling rods. The canvas draught screen fitted between engine and tender can also be seen. This gave some problems in operation owing to its tendency to billow out. The engine is pictured here at the small sub-shed at Pwlhelli awaiting its next duty. It worked in the area for four years and eventually ended up at Carnforth.

27.6.62

Before the introduction of Standard locomotives, the Bedford–St Pancras passenger services were in the hands of 'Compound' 4–4–0s which were rapidly nearing the end of their days. The 75000 series 4–6–0s and 80000 series 2–6–4Ts soon became popular with enginemen. Here, no. 75043 takes on water on shed prior to working to London. This engine ended its days in the north of England, being withdrawn in December 1967.

15.5.55

All eighty of these engines were built at Swindon Works, the first batch of ten going to the Western Region. No. 75001 is seen here with a classmate at Oxford depot. Withdrawals commenced in 1964 with no. 75001 an early casualty, going in that same year. Many of the duties performed by these engines at that time were taken over by diesel multiple units.

31.10.54

No. 75029, pictured here on a gloomy day in a busy engine yard at Oxford, was later to receive a double blastpipe and chimney, considerably changing its appearance. Many readers will recognise this engine as *The Green Knight* which is one of six members of the class to have survived. No. 75029 was fortunate in that it did not have a spell in a scrapyard before being rescued.

31.10.54

No. 75009 was another of the first batch built in 1951 and allocated to the Western Region. Pictured here at Shrewsbury depot, it was at the time allocated to Croes Newydd depot (although it was later to spend a year on the books of Shrewsbury). As with so many of the class it ended up at Carnforth, from where it was withdrawn in the same month that steam finished on British Railways.

21.7.64

Standard no. 75009 has just been coaled at Shrewsbury. The coaling plant was supplied by an inclined siding which can be seen on the left, with an empty coal wagon awaiting removal. Note the large water tank over the coaler, a feature of many Western Region depots.

21.7.64

Fresh from its last general overhaul, no. 75006 stands in the yard at Darlington. The engine is fitted with a double chimney and blastpipe which does little to improve the general appearance. When this picture was taken in 1964 the first examples of the class were about to be withdrawn. No. 75006, despite its overhaul, was withdrawn in August 1967.

2.5.64

The London Midland main line to St Pancras ran close by Bedford depot so passengers could usually see what was standing in the shed yard. Here, no. 75042 of Bedford shed is being moved into position for its next duty, a St Pancras passenger train. Note the interesting gas lamp in this picture and old Departmental coach in the background.

10.7.55

There was a siding at Darlington shed where engines awaiting attention were to be found. No. 75017, a Springs Branch locomotive, is pictured here in company with a WD and another class 4. Shortly after receiving attention, this engine was transferred to Skipton where it was to remain for its last two years in service, mostly used on freight duties. It was withdrawn in January 1967.

2.5.64

Many steam locomotives were to be seen in a grubby external condition in the mid-sixties; the headlong rush to change to diesel power could not come quickly enough for many. No. 75006, allocated to Stoke, had worked into Banbury where this picture was taken. Although it moved in the period before withdrawal in August 1967, it had by this time returned to Stoke.

27.10.65

The Standard 4s were familiar engines at Oxford for several years. No. 75022, which has acquired a double chimney, is standing in the yard completely surrounded by Great Western engines. This engine was to go on to Exmouth Junction for a year before returning to the Western Region where it had started its working days.

9.63

Withdrawn from service, and the coupling rods removed, this is no. 75079 awaiting removal to Woodhams of Barry, South Wales. This engine was among those sent to the Southern Region. It is fitted with the neat Eastleigh-type double chimney and also has a BR1B flush-sided tender with a 7 ton coal capacity, as opposed to the usual pattern of 6 tons. Fortunately it was eventually rescued from Barry.

12.3.67

76000 class 4MT 2–6–0

Introduced: 1952
Total built: 115

Principal dimensions:

Weight:	locomotive	59 tons 15 cwt
	tender	42 tons 3 cwt
Boiler pressure:		225 lb sq. in
Driving wheels:		5 ft 8 in
Tractive effort:		24,170 lb
Cylinders:		17.5 in × 26 in
Walschaerts valve gear		

Number series: 76000–76114. Four of these very versatile 'Moguls' are in preservation.

These engines were basically the well-proven Ivatt class 4 2–6–0 design modified to incorporate BR standard fittings. At the same time the builders took advantage of tests carried out on the Ivatt engines, the Standards incorporating improvements to the blastpipe and chimney. They were mixed traffic locomotives designed to have a wide route availability.

The first 76000 series locomotive was completed at Horwich Works in 1952. Construction of the class took place between 1952 and 1957 at Horwich and Doncaster. No. 76114 was the last new steam locomotive to be built at the latter. Locomotives were supplied new to all regions with the exception of the Western. The Doncaster-built engines sometimes worked as far south as New England on running-in turns. I well recall finding no. 76046 there before it went north to its first shed in Scotland. On another occasion I found no. 76001 of Motherwell depot in ex-works condition at Lincoln, presumably having recently been out-shopped from Doncaster.

These very useful engines were to be found on both passenger and goods workings, with examples on the Southern almost to the last days of steam. Standards of the 73000, 76000, 80000 and 82000 classes were all to be found on the Somerset & Dorset in the final years. The five Stratford-based engines, nos 76030–34, were supplied new in 1953; most of these were to end up stored in the yard at March in the early sixties with their chimneys covered. Also present at this time were a number of stored 'Britannias', plus many other withdrawn engines. The 'Britannias' were moved away for further service on the London Midland Region. The Standard 4MTs were also lucky, finding a new home on the Southern. These particular engines had a recess on the cabside for a tablet exchange mechanism to be fitted. Four of the five were to end up at Guildford, the fifth going to Eastleigh.

Withdrawals commenced in May 1964 with no. 76028 of Eastleigh depot. Six others went that same year. The following year saw another sixteen condemned, and the remaining engines were all withdrawn during 1966/7. The last in service, no. 76084 of Springs Branch, was withdrawn in December 1967, only to join the rows of derelict locomotives at Barry from where it was rescued. Three other examples also survive, all of which spent several years exposed to the elements in South Wales.

Every so often you might come across an unusual engine, often one you least expected, as was the case with no. 76001, ex-works at Doncaster and photographed at Lincoln. This was a Scottish Region engine allocated to Motherwell and would have been running prior to returning to its home depot. It spent its entire working life north of the border, including a spell on the West Highland line, with the last year at Ayr from where it was withdrawn in August 1966.

14.8.55

Doncaster built a large number of the class 4 2–6–0s including no. 76046 which was brand new and undergoing running-in trials when this picture was taken at New England. Construction of this class commenced in 1952 with the last of the 115-strong locomotives being completed in 1957. The final batch went to the London Midland Region. No. 76046 ended its working life at Corkerhill shed.

13.3.55

A work-stained no. 76051 stands at Harston sidings, ready to leave with an iron ore train. This locomotive was at this time allocated to Colwick, Nottingham, but it moved north to Springs Branch for its final few months in service. These engines were based on the well-proven Ivatt design introduced in 1946 but had Standard fittings and modifications.

4.6.66

The first twenty examples of the Standard class 4 2–6–0s were built at Horwich Works in 1952/3. Pictured here at Salisbury, no. 76005 was one of two members of the class allocated to Dorchester shed at this time. Salisbury could always provide plenty of variety in the mid-fifties with a Southern 'Mogul' and Western 'Hall' class also present.

3.9.56

The Standard 4s were a familiar sight north of the border. This is no. 76073 photographed at its home shed, Dumfries; it moved to Ayr in April 1966. Time was running out as just two months later it was withdrawn from service. The high running plate on these locomotives can be clearly seen in this picture. In the background is 'Crab' no. 42914.

9.63

Eastleigh shed had a number of these engines from new in its allocation, including this one, no. 76007, which remained on the Southern Region, ending up at Bournemouth. Several members of the class worked to Weymouth and elsewhere in their final years. Note the steam crane used for handling ash. The cabside carries the BR lion and wheel emblem and is lettered Motive Power Depot Eastleigh.

8.11.55

Doncaster Works built several batches of these locomotives. One batch, numbered 76053–76069, constructed in 1955/6, was fitted with the type BR1B flush-sided tenders for use on the Southern Region. Coal capacity on this type was 7 tons with 4,725 gallons of water. No. 76058 had only been in service for a short time when this picture was taken at Reading, Southern Region shedcode 70E. The locomotive is not carrying a shedplate.

7.8.55

Standard design locomotives were to be found in considerable numbers on the Somerset & Dorset in the mid-sixties. No. 76010 was in the process of being turned at Templecombe shed when this picture was taken. It was allocated to Bournemouth at the time, and just under a year later it was withdrawn.

26.10.65

Four of these Standard 4s were transferred to March depot in 1960. No. 76034 arrived from Norwich the following year. By this time March was in decline and locomotives of several types were stored in various parts of the yard; in due course they were joined by a number of 4MTs. These locomotives had been replaced by diesels, having spent their working life on the Eastern Region. In November 1962 all five were transferred to Brighton.

9.9.62

The last of the five Standard 4MT 2–6–0s to arrive at March was no. 76034, which was transferred from Norwich in September 1961. It was there for just over a year, spending most of the time in store, before all five left for Brighton and further service on the Southern Region. No. 76034 itself spent its final days at Guildford, being withdrawn in September 1964. Note the piece of tarpaulin tied round the chimney in the traditional manner.

9.9.62

This is no. 76034 in store at March. At this time there seemed little hope that it would work again. But the Standards were lucky, and survived the doldrums; after all they were less than ten years old at this time. Note the recess in the cabside for the tablet exchange mechanism that was widely used in parts of East Anglia.

9.9.62

Sights like this were not uncommon in steam days, when locomotives under repair were often to be seen in shed yards. No. 76053 at Weymouth had obviously run into trouble with the bearing of its middle driving wheels: note the rubbing marks on the main frames. At some stage the decision had been made to condemn the engine as it was already withdrawn when this picture was taken.

4.6.67

No. 76006 heads a local passenger train at Brockenhurst. This engine was one of several allocated to Bournemouth at this time. Bournemouth depot closed in July 1967, and its remaining engines were sent for scrap. Steam working finished on the Southern Region at this time. The last locomotive of this design, no. 76084, remained in service at Springs Branch on the London Midland Region until December 1967.

16.9.66

Birkenhead depot was among the last strongholds of steam. No. 76095 was photographed in the shed yard in company with several 9F 2–10–0s. The 4MT was a Chester engine at the time. Built in 1957 at Horwich, it was one of the last members of the class to be constructed and was to manage just ten years service before being withdrawn.

16.10.66

Another picture of no. 76095 at Birkenhead. Steam was approaching its final year, and withdrawn locomotives were to be found at many depots awaiting their final journey to the breaker's yard. Those engines that remained in service often had no number or shed plates, but this was not true of no. 76095 which still has both. Nameplates of 'Britannias' had mostly been removed at this time, and names were sometimes painted on or were non-existent. Everything was geared to dieselisation or electrification on the main lines.

16.10.66

One of the locomotives that was formerly on the Eastern Region but spent some time at March before being transferred to the Southern Region was no. 76033, easily recognisable by the tablet exchange slot cut out on the cabside. The locomotive had already been withdrawn when this picture was taken at Eastleigh. No. 76033 ended its working days at Guildford shed from where it was withdrawn in January 1967.

12.3.67

No. 76066 had just one more month in service when this picture was taken at Eastleigh. This was one of the batch built with the larger BR1B tender. Steam finished on the Southern Region in July 1967. Four members of this class from the 115 built have survived into preservation. Rather surprisingly, only one of the Ivatt 4MT 2–6–0s, no. 43106, survives; this was the design on which the Standard 4MT was based.

4.6.67

77000 class 3MT 2–6–0

Introduced: 1954
Total built: 20

Principal dimensions:

Weight:	locomotive	57 tons 9 cwt
	tender	42 tons 3 cwt
Boiler pressure:		200 lb sq. in
Driving wheels:		5 ft 3 in
Tractive effort:		21,490 lb
Cylinders:		17.5 in × 26 in

Walschaerts valve gear

Number series: 77000–77019. None of this class has survived.

The British Railway Standard class 3MT consisted of just twenty engines. These were not particularly well known, and after running-in trials they were supplied to depots in the North Eastern Region and Scotland. Only in their final years was one allocated to a depot further south for any length of time when no. 77014 arrived at Guildford in March 1966. This engine was the last survivor of the class, being withdrawn in July 1967.

During the planning stage for the Standard designs, there existed a requirement for a class 3MT 2–6–0. In the period between planning and the appearance of the first example, no. 77000, many of the lines for which they were intended had been upgraded by the Civil Engineering Department, opening the way for larger and more powerful class 4 locomotives. (Similar circumstances also applied to the 82000 series 2–6–2Ts introduced in 1952.)

The 3MT engines were certainly not the best looking of the Standard designs, mainly because of the high running plate; nor were they to prove popular with enginemen, soon acquiring a reputation for draughty dirty cabs. All were built at Swindon, the first appearing in 1954. Running-in turns saw them in various parts of the Western Region before they were dispatched to their allocated depots. The first example went to the North Eastern Region, for use mainly on cross-country and branch lines. While perfectly satisfactory on normal routes, their steaming ability was suspect on heavily graded lines such as over Stainmore. Visitors to Darlington during the fifties stood a fair chance of seeing one or more on shed. Several other depots in the region also had examples, but it was the batch allocated to Hurlford depot in Scotland that were the most permanent in the later years.

Diesel locomotives and multiple units were to take over many of their duties in the early sixties. In November 1965 no. 77010, by this time at Stourton, was condemned. In the following year the majority were withdrawn, leaving just three in service at the start of 1967, two at York and no. 77014, by this time at Guildford on the Southern Region, where it caused quite a stir as the only member of the class that many enthusiasts were to see. As is widely known, numerous Southern Region engines were to end up at Woodhams scrapyard, Barry; unfortunately no. 77014 was not among them. If it had been sent there perhaps it would be with us today. Instead its fate was sealed at Birds scrapyard, Risca, in 1968.

The pioneer engine of the series, no. 77000, photographed at Darlington. Less well known than most Standard designs, these engines spent most of their working life in the north-east and Scotland. There was one notable exception, no. 77014, which spent just over a year at Guildford. No. 77000 was withdrawn from Stourton in December 1966.

2.5.64

This twenty-strong class was intended for use on branch and secondary lines. In their early days they took over many of these services in the north-east. After a few years the rapid change-over to diesel railcars reduced their duties. No. 77004, seen here at Darlington, had a number of different sheds in its final years. In 1959 alone it spent short periods at Whitby, Neville Hill, Selby, York and also Scarborough, ending its days at Stourton from where it was withdrawn in December 1966.

8.7.56

This picture of no. 77004, photographed alongside a V2 at Darlington, shows clearly the high running plate. This design was basically the tender version of the 82000 series 2–6–2Ts which had first appeared two years before these engines. It had been intended to construct more 77000 series locomotives but this was cancelled. All twenty examples of the class were built at Swindon.

7.7.56

78000 class 2MT 2–6–0

Introduced: 1952
Total built: 65

Principal dimensions:

Weight:	locomotive	49 tons 5 cwt
	tender	36 tons 17 cwt
Boiler pressure:		200 lb sq. in
Driving wheels:		5 ft 0 in
Tractive effort:		18,515 lb
Cylinders:		16.5 in × 24 in

Walschaerts valve gear

Number series: 78000–78064

Four of these very useful tender locomotives are in preservation. All four were built at Darlington in 1954, nos 78018/19, 78022 and 78059. The latter is in the process of being rebuilt as an example of the class 2 tank version; when complete it will become no. 84030.

The Ivatt 2MT 2–6–0 first appeared in 1946 and was designed for easy maintenance and operation. Self-cleaning smokeboxes, rocking grates and self-emptying ashpans were among its features, plus a modern side-window cab which was immediately popular with enginemen who had been used to working with elderly locomotives, which gave them very little protection especially if working tender first. The Ivatt 2–6–0s were built over a long period. The first batches were built in LMS days at Crewe Works and production continued into the first years after nationalisation. The last Crewe-built engine was no. 46464. In 1951 production of the class was switched to Darlington and in 1952 to Swindon, with the last of the Ivatt 2–6–0s, no. 46527, being completed in 1953.

This well-proven lightweight design was changed to the 78000 series with few alterations except for the incorporation of BR standard fittings. The opportunity was also taken to give a smoother contour to the cab and matching tender cab, at the same time slightly modifying the footplating at the front of the engine.

Production of the Standard engines was moved back to Darlington, where no. 78000 was completed in 1952. In all sixty were built, the last, no. 78064, appearing in 1956. The lightweight 2–6–0s of both the Ivatt and BR Standard series were to be found on many parts of the system, especially on secondary and branch lines, their low axle weight giving them wide route availability. In later days many of these engines were to be found on pilot duties, having been displaced by diesel multiple units. The 78000 series engines were constructed for the Western, Eastern and North Eastern, Scottish and London Midland regions. Withdrawals commenced in 1963, and massive inroads were made in 1965/6, leaving just twelve in service at the start of 1967. The last example was condemned that same year, with none surviving into the final years of steam on British Railways. Four members of the class were sold to Woodhams scrapyard at Barry: nos 78018/19/22 and 78059. The first to leave was no. 78019, which moved to the Severn Valley Railway in 1973. It was followed in due course by the other locomotives, all going to different destinations.

Following the success of the Ivatt lightweight 2MT 2–6–0 introduced in 1946, there was little that needed to be done to the sixty-five Standards 2–6–0s except to bring them into line with BR practice. The two engines in this picture, nos 78055/7, were under construction at Darlington Works, being part of the final batch of ten built in 1956. They both had a comparatively short working life, no. 78055 being withdrawn from Bolton in February 1967 and no. 78057 from Lostock Hall in May 1966.

7.7.56

Construction of no. 78056 nearing completion at Darlington Works. The cab fittings are complete, and work is well under way, with coupling rods, handrails and a few other items still to be added. In the background is another member of the class at an early stage of construction, consisting of just frames and boiler.

7.7.56

The Standard 2MT was used on goods services on the Cambrian line, and several members of the class were allocated to Machynlleth depot. Here, no. 78007 awaits departure from Portmadoc with a goods for Pwllheli. No. 78007 remained at Machynlleth until 1963 when it was transferred to Crewe North, and after several other sheds it was withdrawn from Bolton in May 1967.

27.6.62

Two Standard 2MTs were allocated to Kettering depot, working alongside a number of Ivatt engines on the Cambridge service and various other duties. No. 78020 is seen here leaving St Ives with the afternoon service to Cambridge. Several views of this engine are included, principally because they were taken where no trace of a railway now exists. No. 78020 is about to join the March–Cambridge line for the final section of its journey.

28.8.54

No. 78020 waiting at St Ives for departure to Cambridge. Note the two small boys on the signal-box steps and the nameboard for St Ives Junction. All that remains here now is the former station hotel building, which can just be seen at the end of the train. No. 78020 ended its days at Lostock Hall from where it was withdrawn in May 1967.

28.8.54

One of the Standard 2MTs working on the Mid-Wales line was no. 78003, seen here outside Aberystwyth shed. This was a two-road sub-shed of Machynlleth where the engine was allocated. Note the water crane: many thousands of these existed on British Railways in steam days. No. 78003 was allocated to Shrewsbury for its final year in service, being withdrawn from there in December 1966.

7.61

Another picture of no. 78020, this time on a goods working leaving St Ives on its way to pick up the 'fruit train' which ran in the summer months to northern markets via Kettering. Note the Kettering driver watching me as I took this picture. In the fifties and sixties some photographers were granted lineside permits enabling such shots to be taken.

23.5.53

This locomotive, no. 78027, had no fewer than seven different allocations during the sixties and was on Leicester depot's stock for its final years of service. When this picture was taken at Kettering it was ready to work back. Its end came in September 1965 at a time when huge numbers of engines were being withdrawn and ending up in private scrapyards.

14.3.65

The heaviest train to work over the St Ives–Kettering section was a summer-only fruit train from the Cambridgeshire fruit-growing area around Willingham and Longstanton to northern markets. Prior to the arrival of sufficient numbers of Ivatt 2–6–0s, and later the two Standard versions, it was worked by the ageing Midland 0–6–0s. During the height of the season the train could easily consist of forty or more wagons. Weight restrictions over the River Ouse bridge did not permit double-heading, but a pilot engine waited at Huntingdon East to assist over the steeply graded section to Kettering. No. 78020 was on that duty when this picture was taken. The railway here has long since gone and its route is now given over to the very busy A14.

14.8.54

In the mid-sixties withdrawn locomotives were to be found at many depots, usually minus smokebox and shed plates, as here. No. 78059 was photographed at Crewe South having been condemned several months previously. In the background is another member of the class. However, four Standard 2MTs have made it into preservation. This locomotive is in the process of conversion to a class 2 Standard tank and will, as mentioned, become no. 84030 on completion.

12.2.67

80000 class 4MT 2–6–4T

Introduced: 1951
Total built: 155

Principal dimensions:

Weight:	locomotive	88 tons
Boiler pressure:		225 lb sq. in
Driving wheels:		5 ft 8 in
Tractive effort:		25,100 lb
Cylinders:		18 in × 28 in
Walschaerts valve gear		

Number series: 80000–80154. Fifteen locomotives have survived into preservation, the highest number of all the Standard classes.

The first ten of these very useful 2–6–4Ts were allocated to the Scottish Region. They were built to replace ageing tender locomotives that were then to be found working on many services. These were the forerunners of a 155-strong class introduced in 1951, examples of which were eventually to be found on all regions of British Railways. The overall design work was carried out at Derby, with Doncaster and Swindon being involved in detailed aspects. Construction took place mainly at Brighton although batches were also built at Derby and Doncaster. The final locomotive emerged from Brighton in 1956. These engines conformed to the Universal L1 loading, making them suitable for many routes where the Fairburn 2–6–4Ts could not work.

They were powerful and capable of a fair turn of speed; as might be expected, they soon became popular with enginemen. Principally designed for local passenger suburban workings, for which the design proved to be first class, within a few years they had been overtaken by electrification and the introduction of suburban diesel units.

During the fifties you could not travel far on British Railways, with the exception of the Western Region, before you came across one of these locomotives: on the Midland main line they had taken over the services from 'Compounds' between Bedford and St Pancras; locomotives from Bletchley depot worked through to Cambridge, and were also to be found on the London Tilbury & Southend line; the West Coast main line saw them working suburban services, while in the North Eastern Region they worked branches and services in the Glasgow area. In later years the Western Region used them on the Cambrian line. Gradually they were replaced by more modern motive power and were to find themselves on more mundane duties, especially in the early sixties when the 80000 tanks were to be seen at Clapham Junction working empty stock into and from Waterloo.

One of these engines was to become the first example of the Standard classes to be withdrawn. No. 80103 was condemned in September 1962 after suffering damage. At this time numerous examples of the class and other 2–6–4Ts were in store or found little work. The following year many more were to make their final journey and by 1967 only twenty-five remained in service, with all being withdrawn during the next year. No. 80152 of Eastleigh was the last survivor. Many engines were sold to Woodhams scrapyard, Barry; had this not happened we would not have fifteen examples in preservation. Some were to spend many years at Barry before being rescued. Of those still with us all but one were Brighton-built, the exception being no. 80002 which was constructed at Derby in 1952 and withdrawn from Polmadie in March 1967.

The Standard 4MT 2–6–4Ts were first introduced in 1951. Construction took place at Derby, Brighton and Doncaster, although the latter built just 10 of this 155-strong class. The Doncaster batch consisted of nos 80106–80115, built in 1954. No. 80108 had just been completed and was standing in the yard at Doncaster shed among other ex-works engines, already coaled and watered ready for its running-in trials. The Doncaster batch was destined for the Scottish Region, and no. 80108 was withdrawn from Polmadie in May 1965.

7.11.54

Brighton Works built the highest number of these very useful Standard class 4MT 2–6–4Ts. No. 80088 was in the process of final testing at the works when this picture was taken. Note the cab doorway is partly blocked off: although it was November it was not cold, so the door is probably being used as a wind shield. No. 80088 went to the London Midland Region and was later sent to the Southern Region, being withdrawn from Redhill in June 1965.

14.2.54

Work is well under way on no. 80120 in Brighton Works. The dome is already fitted and the main part of the engine has been painted, lettered, numbered and lined out. There is no sign of its chimney (the one in the foreground belonging to another engine undergoing a general overhaul). In the background T9 class 4–4–0 no. 30719 is receiving attention. No. 80120 spent much of its time in the north-east before going north to Polmadie from where it was withdrawn in May 1967.

25.6.55

The arrival of Standard class 4 2–6–4Ts at Corkerhill sealed the fate of many of the 2P class 4–4–0s used on local passenger services. No. 80009 is about to take its turn under the massive coaling plant at Corkerhill. This engine was one of the first batch built at Brighton in 1951. Its condition suggests it had recently undergone a general overhaul.

26.8.55

One of the largest depots in the Scottish Region was Polmadie, Glasgow, which had some 180 engines allocated to it in the mid-fifties. These included 'Princess Coronation' Pacifics, 'Royal Scots' and numerous ex-Caledonian railway engines. In addition, several of these class 4 tanks were on its books. No. 80115 was the final engine of the Doncaster-built batch and when this picture was taken it was only a few months old. Note the water cranes and numerous lighting poles. No. 80115 was allocated to several Scottish depots in the sixties before returning to Polmadie, from where it was withdrawn in October 1964.

26.8.55

Bournemouth shed was just four months away from closing when this picture of no. 80152 was taken there. Steam finished on the Southern Region in July 1967. The locomotive was in good external condition and carried a white headcode disc with the number 400 on it. This engine was one of the final batch built at Brighton; it was an Eastleigh engine at the time and remained in service until the end of steam.

12.3.67

The Bletchley–Cambridge service, which consisted of four coaches and a horsebox, has just stopped at Sandy behind no. 80083. Horseboxes were once a familiar sight on our railways, as livestock was often moved by rail. The cross-country Bletchley–Cambridge service was worked by 80000 series 2–6–4Ts and 75000 series 4–6–0s at this time. It gave connections to the East Coast and Midland main lines.

31.7.54

Here, the Cambridge–Bletchley train, made up of four coaches of mixed parentage, arrives at Sandy. One could change at Sandy for the East Coast main line but this often involved a lengthy wait as services stopping on the main line were sparse, unlike the situation today. No. 80081 left Bletchley in November 1959 for Willesden, and was later transferred to the Southern, being withdrawn from Bournemouth in June 1965.

31.7.54

Two Standard tank locomotives, both on Bedford's allocation, stand outside the depot. No. 80061 was normally to be seen working the St Pancras services. No. 84005 was used on Northampton and Hitchin trains. No. 80061 spent much of its life on the London Midland Region before going to the Scottish Region at Stirling in March 1960, ending its days along with many of its classmates at Polmadie, from where it was withdrawn in December 1966.

10.10.54

No. 80084 ready to depart with a Cambridge train from platform 7 at Bletchley station. This useful cross-country route during the fifties also carried a considerable amount of freight traffic. The line still remains from Bletchley to Bedford but the remainder has long since been lifted. At the time of writing (1998) consideration is being given to the possibility of reinstating this very useful cross-country line, not from Cambridge to Sandy but off the East Coast main line, replacing the Sandy–Bedford section.

5.9.54

No. 80061 leaving Bedford depot, ready to work a passenger train to St Pancras. For many years the services were worked by 'Compound' 4–4–0s. These powerful tank engines were designed for suburban and local passenger work, in great contrast to the 'Compounds' which were express passenger engines in their heyday and were only relegated to this type of work.

11.9.54

Most of the Bedford 2–6–4Ts were maintained in good external condition, just as the 'Compounds' had been before them. No. 80059 seems to be an exception as it looks in a rather work-stained condition as it moves on to Bedford shed. The piece of ground where I stood to take this picture was an ideal spot from which to photograph engine movements on and off shed as well as on the main line.

21.8.54

The massive signal-box that once stood at the north end of Bletchley station can be clearly seen in this picture. No. 80081 is pictured standing in one of the sidings at Bletchley depot, not in steam and awaiting maintenance. These powerful locomotives had good acceleration and were capable of a fair turn of speed but their working days on suburban services were, in many instances, cut short by electrification and diesel rail cars.

27.2.55

This is the end of the line for no. 80104, pictured here in a siding at Machynlleth depot, together with a classmate and a 2251 class 0–6–0. All had already been withdrawn from service. No. 80104 was lucky as it ended up at Woodhams scrapyard in Barry from where it was rescued after a number of years for preservation.

9.9.65

The final shed for no. 80043 was Templecombe. In this picture the engine is seen leaving with a passenger train amid clouds of steam. It certainly had a good head of steam, as can be seen from the safety valves. No. 80043 had only a matter of months left in service, being withdrawn in March 1966. Massive inroads were made into the remaining locomotives that year, and only twenty-five made it into 1967.

26.10.65

Standard class 4 2–6–4Ts had been a familiar sight on the Southern Region since they were first introduced and were also still to be found at Nine Elms and other depots when steam finished. Here, no. 80010 rattles past Clapham Junction. It was allocated to Three Bridges depot at the time, ending its days in June 1964 at Brighton.

9.61

No 80000 series 2–6–4Ts were allocated to Eastleigh shed in the mid-fifties although they were frequently seen there. Here, no. 80016 is pictured with 'Lord Nelson' class no. 30861 *Lord Anson*, both having arrived on shed for servicing. Eastleigh was at this time home to several of the 82000 series 2–6–2Ts.

8.11.55

This is no. 80016 again, this time at Bricklayers Arms depot when it was just a few weeks old. The fireman appears to be standing on the far side tank and peering through the filler cap for some reason. No. 80016 spent its working life on the Southern Region and was withdrawn from Eastleigh at the end of steam in July 1967.

1.11.51

The south end bay platform at Cambridge was used by the Bletchley trains. For years these were worked by Stanier & Fairburn 2–6–4Ts until the introduction of the Standards. Here, no. 80042 is awaiting departure with a morning service. This engine was transferred from Bletchley in December 1959, spending its last years on the Southern Region. 22.8.53

This is no. 80017 of Tunbridge Wells, pictured at Bricklayers Arms depot, London. Note the white headcode with the number 659. The Southern Region received the second batch of these engines, which were first built at Brighton. Nos 80010–19 spent their working lives on this region, and in later years others that were surplus to requirements elsewhere were sent to join them. No. 80017 was a fairly early withdrawal, going in September 1964. 25.11.54

Another Standard 4MT 2–6–4T at Bricklayers Arms in November 1954 was no. 80011, also from Tunbridge Wells, these engines having a regular working to London. This one remained in service right to the end of steam on the Southern Region, its final shed being Bournemouth. In the background is 'Schools' class no. 30907 *Dulwich*.

25.11.54

Numerous special trains were organised during the last years of steam. 'The Blue Belle' was one of these. No. 80084, seen here at Haywards Heath, piloted the newly restored E4 no. 473 *Birch Grove* from Victoria to the Bluebell Railway, its new home. The immaculate Standard class 4MT was allocated at this time to 75D Horsham. In the background can be seen the Adams Radial tank no. 488.

31.3.63

Quite a number of these engines spent their final years at Nine Elms, where their duties included empty stock workings into and out of Waterloo station, which for many years had been in the hands of elderly M7 class 0–4–4Ts. Here, no. 80012 is ready to depart from Clapham Junction. This engine remained at Nine Elms until withdrawal in March 1967.

3.3.66

Looking at this picture of no. 80144 it is difficult to believe that in just two months it would be withdrawn from service. This engine spent a short period at Nine Elms, being transferred there from Eastleigh in February 1966, and was withdrawn in May. Here, no. 80144 shunts stock at Clapham Junction. This was one of the batch built at Brighton in 1956 and it managed just ten years service.

3.3.66

No. 80134 of Bournemouth shed ambles along near Wareham with a lightweight goods in 1966. There was less than a year of steam working left on the Southern Region at this time. No. 80134 remained in service at Bournemouth until the bitter end. Having spent some of its life on the London Tilbury line, based at Plaistow and Tilbury depot, it left there for Swansea East Dock in August 1962, before moving to the Southern in July 1964.

16.9.66

No. 80085 takes water at Brockenhurst while working the Lymington service. This engine has already lost its front number plate. The Standard 4MTs were to be found at several Southern Region depots in the final years of steam working.

16.9.66

82000 class 3MT 2–6–2T

Introduced: 1952
Total built: 45

Principal dimensions:

Weight:	locomotive	74 tons 1 cwt
Boiler pressure:		200 lb sq. in
Driving wheels:		5 ft 3 in
Tractive effort:		21,490 lb
Cylinders:		17.5 in × 26 in
Walschaerts valve gear		

Number series: 82000–82044

This is another class which has no survivors. Originally built for light passenger work, these engines would have been ideal motive power for many preserved lines.

These mixed traffic locomotives were designed principally for passenger work and my first opportunity to photograph one, no. 82014, came at Eastleigh in November 1955. In the early sixties I recorded this same engine on Waterloo to Clapham Junction stock workings, in company with several classmates, and again with other members of the class from Nine Elms at Cohens scrapyard, Kettering, in late 1964.

The 82000 class consisted of forty-five engines introduced in 1952, all being built at Swindon between 1952 and 1955. They were principally built to work over routes having a 16 ton axle loading and requiring more powerful locomotives than the existing 2MT design. In time this requirement was considerably reduced by the upgrading of various lines, enabling the more numerous class 4 engines to operate them. During the fifties these engines displaced many older designs and could be seen on the Exmouth branch, the Penrith–Darlington line and many others. In the late fifties they were introduced to the Somerset & Dorset and in the early sixties to Machynlleth, taking them among other places to Portmadoc and Pwlheli. They remained on the S & D into its final steam years, the last being withdrawn in December 1965, although in general they were less successful than some of the other standard designs.

In their final years a number of these engines were transferred to Nine Elms, principally to work empty stock to and from Clapham Junction. Steam was already running down, and they and the other Standards used on this work were usually in very poor external condition.

Withdrawals started in 1964 and around the middle of the year included the first of the Nine Elms engines, several of which were sold to Cohens, Kettering. At the start of 1966 just sixteen remained in service, but not for long as only two survived into 1967, both at Nine Elms. This is another case of 'if only': if any examples had found their way to Barry, perhaps there would still be a survivor. Instead this was one of the four Standard classes to become extinct.

No. 82014 has just taken water at Eastleigh depot, and something on the locomotive would appear to be causing concern to the driver and running foreman, both visible behind the water crane. This particular locomotive, in company with others of the class, spent its last two years of service at Nine Elms working stock in and out of Waterloo in company with Standard class 4 2–6–4Ts and class 5 4–6–0s.

8.11.55

The Standard 3MT 2–6–2Ts were used on services in Mid-Wales where they replaced Great Western types; this is no. 82020 pictured at Portmadoc. This engine was one of a number allocated to Machynlleth depot at this time; it was to remain here until April 1965 when it was sent to join classmates allocated to Nine Elms. Its period there was short-lived, and it was withdrawn from service just five months later.

25.6.62

The Standard 2–6–2Ts performed much useful work on the Mid-Wales line. No. 82008 had only recently been transferred to Machynlleth when this picture was taken at Barmouth and the locomotive still carries the shed plate of its former depot, 85A Worcester. It was among the first to be withdrawn, being one of three condemned in 1964, at which time it was allocated to Taunton depot.

7.61

No. 82041 has a good head of steam with plenty more escaping as it stands in cold grey conditions at Bath Green Park station, ready to work a local passenger service on the Somerset & Dorset. Time was running out for this engine as just two months later it was withdrawn from service. Standard classes were widely used on the S & D in its final years of steam working. Even the massive 9F 2–10–0s were to be seen on passenger services.

26.10.65

The end of Clapham Junction station was a good place to photograph the locomotives employed on stock workings to and from Waterloo station. For years M7 0–4–4Ts were a familiar sight on these duties, but by the early sixties Standard designs had replaced them. No. 82018 arrives with empty stock; note the platelayer watching carefully near the first coach – with electrified track these engineering staff had to be very careful.

3.3.66

Just one month after withdrawal from Bristol (Bath Road) shed, no. 82037 was in Cashmores scrapyard at Newport. Locomotives awaiting their final journey, some of which were quite lengthy, to a scrap merchant were a fairly common sight. In most yards they were not there for long before being cut up. Thankfully, there was, of course, one notable exception – Woodhams of Barry.

25.10.65

Most of the Standard 3MTS which spent their last working days based at Nine Elms ended up at Cohens scrapyard, Kettering, based in an old ironstone quarry at Cransley. Here, no. 82025 and a classmate are waiting for work to begin. Several Southern Region locomotives were cut up here, including W class 2–6–4Ts and at least one 'Schools' class 4–4–0. Wagons and coaches also arrived in large numbers, and the remains of one of the former can be seen lying on its side behind the engine.

13.12.64

Surrounded by the remains of scrapped locomotives, Standard 3MT no. 82012 awaits a similar fate at Cohens scrapyard. This was one of the members of the class transferred to Nine Elms for stock workings. Just thirteen years old when condemned, it would normally have been in service for many more years, but the modernisation plan had resulted in a headlong rush to get rid of steam.

31.1.65

Locomotive scrapyards sprang up in many parts of the country during the sixties; prior to this withdrawn engines were cut up at a railway works where the scrap roads were always a point of interest for enthusiasts. Cohens at Kettering cut up many examples of several Standard classes as well as a small number of industrial locomotives from Oxfordshire ironstone workings. No. 82011, a classmate and the Western Region pannier tank engine would have been reduced to a pile of scrap metal within days of this picture being taken.

3.1.65

84000 class 2MT 2–6–2T

Introduced: 1953
Total built: 30

Principal dimensions:

Weight:	locomotive	63 tons 5 cwt
Boiler pressure:		200 lb sq. in
Driving wheels:		5 ft 0 in
Tractive effort:		18,515 lb
Cylinders:		16.5 in × 24 in
Walschaerts valve gear		

Number series: 84000–84029

No examples survive of this class which was basically the Ivatt 2MT with BR fittings. Four of the earlier Ivatt engines are in preservation.

When Ivatt introduced his 2MT lightweight 2–6–0 in 1946 it was accompanied by a tank version that was eventually to become a class of 130 locomotives, the last batch being built at Derby in 1952. As with the tender locomotives, it was a highly successful design.

The following year no. 84000, the first of the Standard 2MTs, appeared. The first twenty locomotives were built at Crewe. Another batch of ten was ordered from Darlington Works destined for the Southern Region in 1957, bringing the class total to thirty. These were fitted with vacuum control gear for motor train working and were intended to replace older designs still working on branch lines and secondary services. The equipment was removed from many of them in the sixties, their requirement on branch duties being over.

The Ivatt 2–6–0s were first introduced to Kettering depot to work the Cambridge service, and although this shed never received a tank version there were examples at nearby depots. On at least one occasion one worked through to Huntingdon with an Engineers Inspection Saloon. On several occasions during the fifties I visited Bedford, usually finding no. 84005 in the yard on each visit. This engine had a long association with the depot, although it was for short periods transferred away, returning in February 1963 for the last time, after which it alternated between Wellingborough and Leicester, from where it was withdrawn in October 1965.

Several examples of the class were to be found in North Wales during the early sixties, but work was hard to find for these and other smaller engines and on occasions examples were stored at Llandudno Junction shed. In 1963 the axe fell on no. 84012 of Southport, to be followed by quite a number in 1964; the twenty remaining at the start of 1965 were all withdrawn in that same year. Surprisingly the Standards were outlived by quite a number of the Ivatt engines, the last examples of which were not withdrawn until 1967.

Although no examples of the Standards have survived, no. 78058, one of the tender engines, is in the process of being rebuilt into a tank version on the Bluebell Railway. When completed it will become no. 84030.

The 84000 series 2MT 2–6–2Ts were basically the earlier Ivatt design modified with British Railways Standard fittings. Only thirty were built, in two batches. No. 84009 was one of the first constructed at Crewe in 1953. It was only three years old when this picture was taken at Royston. The engine is fitted with vacuum control gear for motor-train working. This locomotive moved about considerably in its final years, from Hull (Dairycoates), Llandudno Junction, Croes Newydd and finally back to Llandudno in June 1964, from where it was scrapped the following year.

24.6.56

Locomotives for repair were often to be found at the back of Bletchley shed. These were not just engines allocated to the depot, as on many occasions express locomotives that had failed in the area often received attention. No. 84002 was a Bletchley locomotive which remained there until condemned in April 1965. The vacuum control gear can be clearly seen in this picture.

9.5.65

Standard 2MT no. 84005 had a long association with Bedford depot, mostly working on motor-train services in the area alongside Ivatt 2–6–2Ts. It did have a number of breaks, going to Neasden on two occasions, albeit for short periods. It was also allocated to Kentish Town for six months and spent time at Wellingborough and Leicester, from where it was withdrawn in October 1965.

10.10.54

No. 84005 again, photographed ten years later inside the roundhouse at Wellingborough depot. The engine is in good external condition. Shortly after this picture was taken it left for its final depot, Leicester, and the following October it was withdrawn. Note the large smoke-hoods suspended from the shed roof. As the 2MT was receiving attention, the chimney was not under the adjacent hood.

8.11.64

By the mid-fifties many of the small tank locomotives previously used on branch services were lying idle, their place taken by diesel railcars. Here, no. 84003 is out to grass with an Ivatt 2–6–2T at Llandudno Junction depot. A month after this picture was taken no. 84003 was condemned and towed away for scrapping.

10.9.65

In the years leading up to the end of steam working, locomotives were often to be seen in a terrible external condition. No. 84006 was in its final year when this picture was taken at Wellingborough. No one bothered much about steam any more as diesels had become the usual motive power and for many people the sooner steam went the better. All that was to be found at this shed at this time were a few 8F and 9F 2–10–0s, plus a large number of diesels.

25.4.65

92000 class 9F 2–10–0

Introduced: 1954
Total built: 251

Principal dimensions:

Weight:	locomotive	86 tons 14 cwt
	tender	52 tons 10 cwt
Boiler pressure:		250 lb sq. in
Driving wheels:		5 ft 0 in
Tractive effort:		39,670 lb
Cylinders:		20 in × 28 in
Walschaerts valve gear		

Number series: 92000–92250

No. 92220 *Evening Star* was the last steam locomotive built at Swindon Works and for British Railways. Completed with double copper capped chimney and painted in BR fully lined green livery, it was scheduled from new to be preserved as part of the National Collection.

Nos 92020–92029 were built at Crewe Works in 1955 with the latest type of Franco-Crosti boiler, in the hope of achieving worthwhile savings on coal consumption. After just three years most were in store as a result of high maintenance requirements and corrosion, having largely failed to come up to expectations regarding coal savings. In 1959 rebuilding commenced, still retaining the smaller boiler and firebox but with normal draughting arrangements.

It was not until 1954 that the last Standard design appeared. The 9F 2–10–0 heavy freight locomotives were without doubt one of the most successful of all the designs, and eventually totalled 251, including the last steam engine built for British Railway. The original plans for a heavy goods engine were for a 2–8–2 design, but this was changed to 2–10–0; this wheel arrangement was not unknown as twenty-five of the ex-WD Austerity locomotives had been purchased by British Railways and were at work in the Scottish Region. Nevertheless this wheel arrangement was alien to this country generally, as was the 2–8–2; the two Gresley P2 class 2–8–2s had been withdrawn in LNER days. Over the years the 2–8–0 and 0–8–0 designs had become widely accepted as the norm for heavy goods duties. The Standard classes generally showed little variation, with the class 5 an exception, some being built with Caprotti valve gear. The 9Fs were the most interesting in this respect. The first example was completed at Crewe works in 1954, and was certainly very different from the existing heavy goods engines with their massive proportions, ten coupled driving wheels, smoke deflectors and 9F power rating. As with almost all new designs, some teething troubles were experienced, notably with the brakes. Several members of the class were allocated to New England depot where their duties included heavy coal trains to Ferme Park, London. Braking trials were conducted at two places between Peterborough and London, the first at Huntingdon after the long descent of 1 in 200. Another problem was that the regulator tended to stick at slow speed. Once these difficulties were overcome the 9Fs soon proved themselves to be very capable on the heaviest trains.

One batch of engines, originally intended to be of the conventional type, was the subject of a decision to try out Crosti boilers; it was hoped this might result in coal economies. Construction was held up until the necessary design work was completed and they finally appeared from Crewe Works in 1955. All were allocated to Wellingborough shed for use on the Midland main line. These engines were very different in appearance, the exhaust coming out halfway along the boiler side; what appeared to be a normal chimney was in fact only used for lighting up, after which it was closed. These engines did not find favour with the enginemen, and complaints were soon received regarding the extremely unpleasant cab conditions with smoke and steam swirling around; in an effort to improve this and visibility generally, smoke deflector plates were fitted around the exhaust. Another problem was corrosion in various parts of the system. Worse still was the fact that the anticipated savings in coal consumption were not there. These engines became hated by the crews and were soon to be found standing around in the shed yard pending a decision as to their future. Eventually, it was decided to remove the Crosti equipment, although retaining the reduced proportions boiler and firebox but with normal draughting. Another notable difference from the Standard 9Fs was that no smoke deflectors were fitted. These former Crosti engines were also less powerful.

The original 9Fs were delivered with a single chimney. In 1957 no. 92178 was completed with a double blastpipe and chimney, and trials on the Western Region and at the Swindon test plant showed an increase in power and a saving on coal consumption. From no. 92183 the 9Fs were constructed with this modification. As with all rules there was an exception, no. 92250, of which more later. Rather surprisingly, only a few of the earlier locomotives were to receive the double chimney, and it was regarded that in normal service there was little to choose between them.

Another notable experiment that took place in 1958 was the fitting of mechanical stoking to nos 92165–7 of the American Berkley design. These engines required a supply of specially crushed coal. A gain of evaporation was the result but with increased coal consumption. These engines ran in this condition until 1962 when they were converted to hand-firing. One of these engines, no. 92167, was to have the distinction of being the last 9F in normal revenue service, being withdrawn from Carnforth in June 1968 and scrapped by Campbells of Airdrie.

The final experiment took place in 1959 when no. 92250 was fitted with a Giesl oblong ejector, the normal double chimney being removed and replaced with the flat Giesl type. The purpose was to find out if increased power could be obtained from a given fuel consumption, ideally using poor grade coal. This system was the invention of Dr Giesl-Giselingen of Austria. Results were disappointing and no more locomotives were converted although the system remained on no. 92250 throughout its short life. It was withdrawn from Gloucester Horton Road in December 1965, coinciding with the end of steam on the Western Region. It was sold to Cashmores of Newport and cut up.

For many years the massive Midland Railway 0–10–0 nicknamed 'Big Bertha' banked trains on the notorious 1 in 37 Lickey incline. When this locomotive was withdrawn, no. 92079 was fitted with a large electric headlamp and worked on this duty assisted by various other locomotives, including 9Fs at times. Presenting an even more formidable gradient was the 1 in 35 encountered by the Tyne Dock to Consett iron ore trains. For many years these were made up of bogie 56 ton hopper wagons with air pumps to operate the doors, and were worked by North Eastern Q7 0–8–0s and 01 class 2–8–0s. Ten 9Fs were allocated to Tyne Dock shed for this work, and were fitted with Westinghouse pumps on the footplate situated over the centre pair of driving wheels. They presented a splendid sight when they were working hard, the train engine assisted by another banking.

While designed for heavy goods work the 9Fs were certainly not unknown on passenger trains, and they were to become particularly well known on the difficult route of the Somerset & Dorset. A small stud was allocated to Bath Green Park shed principally for working heavy weekend services and specials. There are many other instances elsewhere recording these locomotives on passenger trains, often at short notice. Passenger working was restricted to the summer months as these engines had no provision for steam heating. Parcels and pigeon traffic were other duties they took in their stride.

The Standard 9Fs were built at Crewe and Swindon Works, and a 9F had the distinction of being the last Swindon-built steam engine and the final one constructed for British Railways. This engine was no. 92220 *Evening Star*. During its early years this locomotive was frequently seen on passenger trains. Completed in March 1960, this magnificent engine completed just five years service, being withdrawn from Cardiff East Dock shed in March 1965. There are eight other 9Fs in preservation. No. 92203, now named *Black Prince*, went straight to its new owner but all the rest ended up at Woodhams scrapyard, Barry, from where they were eventually rescued after a long period of exposure to the elements.

My first opportunity to photograph a 9F at rest was no. 92042 at its home shed, New England. These engines replaced some of the depot's WD 2–8–0s. The first arrivals experienced some troubles with braking, and a series of trials was conducted at Huntingdon and another location near London. Once the problems were resolved, 9Fs were a very familiar sight right up to the end of steam working.

13.3.55

This is no. 92042 again, seven years later, at the head of a long train of coal empties from Ferme Park. Given the main line on its journey northwards, the driver is opening up the engine for the long drag to Abbots Ripton. No. 92042 ended its days at Colwick in December 1965.

4.10.62

The Standard 9F 2–10–0 was a very successful design. Although they were intended for heavy freight working they were capable of a fair turn of speed, and on occasions were used for parcels, pigeons and passenger trains, especially in the final years of steam on the Somerset & Dorset during the summer months. Here, no. 92040 of New England is seen in full cry at the head of a long train of empties.

14.3.63

When these locomotives were introduced to the Midland main line they soon replaced the Beyer-Garratts, and 9Fs and Stanier 8F 2–8–0s monopolised the heavy goods workings. Wellingborough depot received both conventional 9Fs and those with Crosti boilers, the latter introduced as a coal-saving measure, supplies being critical at this time. They were not a success and were later rebuilt. No. 92016 was a Wellingborough engine, and is seen here with its classmates and the well-known Stanier 'Eight Freights'.

27.3.55

Most parcel trains on the East Coast main line were worked by Gresley V2 2–6–2s. On occasions, Pacifics and Standard 9Fs appeared on these workings, as was the case in this photograph as no. 92146 approaches Huntingdon en route for Kings Cross, having taken over the train at Peterborough.

4.10.62

No. 92188, one of the class fitted with a double chimney, heading a fast goods train passes the first of the Huntingdon Down line travelling post office lineside installations. The warning board, dispatching arms and receiving net can be clearly seen in this picture. After several years at New England no. 92188 finished its days at Colwick depot.

13.6.57

Only ten of these locomotives, nos 92020–92029, were built with Franco-Crosti boilers; all ten were allocated to Wellingborough depot where they soon became highly unpopular, so much so that moves were made to get them transferred somewhere else, but without success. The exhaust on these engines was situated halfway along the right-hand-side of the boiler and a faint trace of smoke can be seen in this picture of no. 92028. These engines were principally disliked for their unpleasant working conditions, and a smoke deflector was later fitted in an effort to prevent smoke drifting on to the footplate.

22.7.56

Franco-Crosti 9F no. 92026 prepares to leave Wellingborough depot. This picture shows the position of the exhaust chimney. The chimney in the conventional position was only used for steam raising, after which it was blanked off. Due to the problems they encountered, examples of the class were soon to be seen lying idle and awaiting conversion. No. 92026 was the first to be rebuilt, in late 1959, the rest all being rebuilt over a three-year period.

22.7.56

This view of no. 92026 shows the left-hand-side of the engine, the main boiler barrel and the pre-heater drum below. This design was the invention of Piero Crosti, and claims were made that savings of nearly 20 per cent could be made on coal consumption. However, the engines could not meet these expectations. After rebuilding nine were to remain in service until 1967, the exception, no. 92028, being withdrawn in October 1966.

2.7.56

Rebuilt Crosti 9F no. 92023, photographed at Birkenhead. The pre-heater drum has been removed and replaced by a conventional system. In rebuilt form they retained the same boiler and were never fitted with smoke deflectors. Their smaller boiler size meant they were less powerful and so they were classified 8F. No. 92023 had just one year's service left when this picture was taken.

16.10.66

One of the rebuilt Crosti 9Fs, no. 92020, pictured at Kettering depot. In its final years this engine was allocated to several depots, ending up at Birkenhead from where it was withdrawn in October 1967. Although rebuilt these engines still retained their basic outline. Gone were the problems of smoke, fumes and steam entering the footplate, which had created dangerous and extremely unpleasant conditions for the enginemen.

13.12.64

In 1955 a number of 9Fs were fitted with Westinghouse pumps and sent to Tyne Dock shed. These pumps were to operate the hopper doors on iron ore wagons. More engines were fitted with the pumps and followed in 1956. No. 92064 is seen here outside Tyne Dock shed, its pumps clearly visible midway along the footplating. Prior to the arrival of the 9Fs, 01 class 2–8–0s and a few Q7 0–8–0s worked these trains over the steeply graded line between Tyne Dock and Consett.

7.7.56

New England shedcode had changed from 35A to 34E by the time this picture was taken in 1961. Here, no. 92188 heads north with a van train at Huntingdon. On an adverse gradient little effort was required from the engine. 9Fs were the principal class remaining at New England when it closed to steam in January 1965.

24.8.61

No. 92040 approaches Huntingdon with a loaded train of sixteen Prestflow cement wagons. An 'Up slow' track had been laid between Abbots Ripton and Huntingdon at this time, but the station area still presented a bottleneck. Despite the considerable work involved in installing this line, it was later removed.

21.9.61

These engines had a long association with March depot, working in with heavy freights to and from the massive Whitemoor marshalling yards. No. 92140 was a New England engine. Steam was running down when this picture was taken, as ever-increasing numbers of diesels were being delivered. In its heyday March would have been crowded with heavy freight locomotives on a Sunday.

23.6.63

March depot lost its steam allocation in November 1963 but for months afterwards steam locomotives were still to be seen here, mostly visitors from the London Midland Region and northern sheds. Visitors never knew quite what to expect. No. 92122, a Wellingborough engine, is standing over the ashpits, once a very busy spot. In the background is Stanier 5MT 2–6–0 no. 42951.

25.10.64

The overhead water filling arrangements at New England make this location instantly recognisable. Closure was only a matter of five months away. The most numerous class to be found there at this time was the 9F 2–10–0s; here, no. 92181 and a classmate, its number obscured by grime, stand ready for their next duty. On closure, serviceable locomotives were transferred away but it was the end of the road for no. 92181, officially condemned in February 1965.

30.8.64

Despite the appearance of no. 92123 at Kettering it had recently received works attention and was still in reasonable external condition. The smokebox door number plate has gone and the number has been chalked on. In the background can be seen an unusual visitor: B1 4–6–0 no. 61240 *Harry Hinchliffe* was still in service and not destined for the nearby scrapyard.

13.12.64

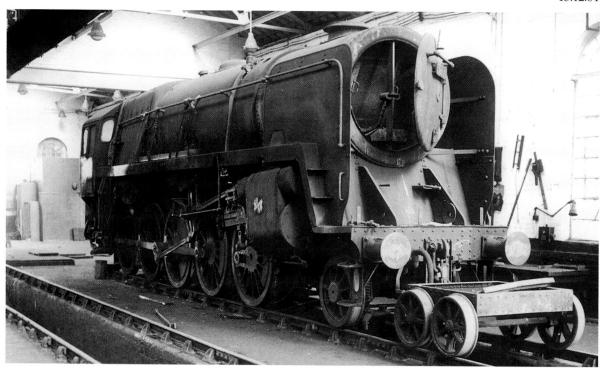

No. 92171, in a terrible external condition, awaits attention in the small repair shop attached to New England shed. The front coupling rods have been removed and part of the valve gear dismantled. This engine had already been condemned and was in the process of being made ready for towing away to a scrapyard, confirmed by the coupling rod already tied on top of the running plate.

30.8.64

Although New England was still a few weeks from closure, already withdrawn locomotives were to be seen in the yard as was the case with no. 92176 which had been withdrawn six months before this picture being taken. This locomotive would soon be prepared for its final journey. Note the massive coaling plant in the background, which by this time was used only occasionally.

6.12.64

Visitors still worked in to New England daily in its final months of steam. No. 92164 was a Saltley engine. It has already been serviced and awaits its return working to the Birmingham area. In the background is one of several old tenders to be seen there in use on sludge carriers and snow ploughs.

30.8.64

The home depot of no. 92246 was Severn Tunnel Junction. As can easily be seen from this picture, it was in a terrible condition when photographed at Banbury depot. A month after this picture was taken it was transferred to its final shed, Gloucester Horton Road, from where it was withdrawn after just two months in December 1965, the shed closing at that time and all remaining engines going for scrap.

27.10.65

Judging by the comments chalked on the cabside of no. 92131 at Kettering, this engine was awaiting attention to the brick arch. This picture clearly shows the pipework in front of and below the cab, as well as the middle pair of driving wheels which were flangeless. No. 92131 was allocated to Westhouses depot at the time, but later moved north to Speke Junction and finally Birkenhead.

8.64

On this visit to Kettering I found several 9Fs present; a number were Wellingborough engines, such as no. 92102, but others came from much farther afield. In the final years of steam many of these engines were transferred to Birkenhead when their duties were taken over by diesels. No. 92102 was one of these, being withdrawn in November 1967.

8.64

This picture has been included as it shows details of the 9F cylinders and valve gear. The locomotive, no. 92102, is in a far from clean condition although the working parts were not covered in too much grease and grime at the time.

8.64

No. 92205, a York engine, was just seven years old when this picture was taken at Normanton, but it had just fifteen months service left, a victim of the headlong rush into dieselisation. It is pictured coupled to a type BR1 G tender.

20.3.66

Nearly home, New England 9F no. 92171 rumbles past Walton, Peterborough, with a long mixed freight. The train would run into the extensive sidings at Westwood, the locomotive being released for servicing, and in due course another engine worked the train forward after any marshalling (and sorting if required) had been done.

6.9.62

The boiler of no. 92123 seems to have received the residue from a water softening plant somewhere; in due course no doubt this became less visible as a coating of grime accumulated. This picture also gives a good idea of the length of these engines which overall amounted to 66 ft 2 in.

15.11.64

The Standard 9F was the last of the Standard designs to make its appearance, and was unquestionably one of the most successful. In all 251 were built between 1954 and 1960. No. 92106 was photographed at Wellingborough in a typical work-stained condition.

14.3.65

Wellingborough depot could still provide Stanier 8F and Standard 9F 2–10–0s in 1965, one of which, no. 92106, was a visitor from Leicester in 1965. By this time many diesels were already in evidence, one of which can be clearly seen in the background. The 9Fs would normally have been expected to provide thirty or more years' service in steam days, and the cost of their very short working lives is almost incalculable.

14.3.65

Some idea of the size of the 9F design can be gauged by comparison with the 2800 class no. 3855 pictured alongside no. 92137 at Banbury. No. 92137 was a visitor from Saltley depot. It was allocated to the depot for a number of years, in August 1966 moving to Croes Newydd for just four months before transferring to Carlisle Kingmoor for its last ten months in service.

9.63

No. 92006 started life fitted with a single chimney, but was one of the four locomotives to receive a double chimney during service. A considerable number of 9Fs were supplied new with the double blastpipe and chimney; these were nos 92178 and 92183–92250. This picture of no. 92006 was taken at York, its home depot at the time, having moved there in 1963 from Newport, South Wales. In October 1966 it was on the move again, for the last time, to Wakefield, being withdrawn in April 1967.

2.5.64

York shed was still very interesting in 1964 with a surprising number of locomotive types in evidence, including Pacifics of classes A1 and A3, WDS, B1s, V2s, K1s and even occasional representatives of the North Eastern J27 class 0–6–0s. Several Standard class 9F locomotives were also allocated to the depot. No. 92179 was a visitor, having worked in from New England, Peterborough.

2.5.64

The double blastpipe and chimney fitted to some 9Fs was, in the opinion of many, the most suitable. No. 92190, seen here at March, was a visitor from Colwick. Long since gone were the days of a long stream of engines awaiting coaling at the plant seen in the background. Very few locomotives were still allocated to March at this time, the depot being just seven months from losing its entire allocation.

23.6.63

March depot had lost its own allocation of steam locomotives fourteen months before this picture was taken. Steam continued to arrive on heavy goods trains for a considerable time afterwards, some working in from a great distance, as was the case with no. 92206 of York depot. When new in May 1959, this engine went to the Western Region and later the Southern at Eastleigh, where it worked 1,200 ton trains from the Fawley oil terminal to Totton. When this duty finished, the engine went on to Feltham, then York and finally Wakefield; it was withdrawn in May 1967 when it was just eight years old.

28.2.65

The north end of New England shed presented a sad sight in August 1964, with only a handful of locomotives remaining. The numerous sidings in the fifties would have been packed with engines, especially on a Sunday. No. 92149 is pictured ready for the road; behind it stands one of the last remaining Ivatt 4MT 2–6–0s at the depot.

30.8.64

Carnforth depot on a wet gloomy day in March 1968. No. 92223 was just one month from withdrawal. No. 92004 in the background had already completed its working life. The final steam locomotives had just five months to go and many enthusiasts flocked to the area in the final months.

17. 3. 68

During the final years of steam the majority of withdrawn locomotives were cut up by private scrapyards. Cashmores of Newport were fairly quick to deal with engines as they arrived. No. 92237 had only been withdrawn from Newport (Ebbw Junction) the previous month, but already was within days of the end. The coupling rods and valve gear are still intact, no doubt owing to the short distance involved (although it may even have worked there under its own steam).

25.10.65

Someone at Wellingborough evidently thought no. 92101 had some working life left, and thus it was placed in store with the chimney covered. As it happens they were correct: the engine moved shortly after this picture was taken to Birkenhead where it remained in service for just over two years.

25.4.65

Barry scrapyard, October 1965. No. 92207 is still remarkably intact; the cab windows and some fittings near the cab had gone but the coupling rods and valve gear are still in place. This 1959 Swindon-built engine was one of the lucky ones. After many years exposed to the elements it was purchased for preservation, going to a new home on the East Lancashire Railway where it was named *Morning Star*. In all nine 9Fs still survive including *Evening Star*, which is part of the National Collection.

25.10.65

The last new steam locomotive built for British Railways at Swindon Works was no. 92220 *Evening Star*, completed in March 1960. This locomotive was turned out with a Great Western-type copper cap to the chimney and in full green passenger livery. Its first depot was Cardiff Canton where it was often used on passenger trains; it left there in August 1962 for Bath (Green Park) where it was used on the S & D. In October 1962 it moved to Old Oak Common for just one month before going to Oxford and then back to Bath in August 1963, two months later moving to its final shed, Cardiff East Dock, from where it was withdrawn in March 1965. It was just five years old. It was scheduled for eventual preservation from new. This picture was taken in Crewe paint shops. After working many special trains it is currently at the National Railway Museum York.

16.10.66

EX-WAR DEPARTMENT (AUSTERITY) LOCOMOTIVES

WD (Austerity) class 8F 2–8–0

Introduced: Ministry of Supply Design 1943
Total taken into BR stock: 733

Principal dimensions:

Weight:	locomotive	70 tons 5 cwt
	tender	55 ton 10 cwt
Boiler pressure:		225 lb sq. in
Driving wheels:		4 ft 8.5 in
Tractive effort:		34,215 lb
Cylinders:		19 in × 28 in

Walschaerts valve gear

Number series: 90000–90732. Only one of these locomotives was named, no. 90732 *Vulcan*. Despite the fact that the last of the locomotives taken into British Railways stock remained in service until 1967, none made it into preservation.

The ex-WD 2–8–0s were to be found on all regions of British Railways in the fifties. Those locomotives allocated to the Western were easily recognisable as they were fitted with a top feed cover and a fire irons compartment on the running plate. Wherever there was a considerable amount of heavy mineral traffic you would find WDs, so much so that many enthusiasts of the day paid little attention to them. Whenever they received a works overhaul they would come back with a shiny coat of black paint, which would start to disappear under a layer of grime within a matter of days. In their final years these engines were often covered with a considerable accumulation of soot, grease and grime. No one even thought about cleaning them. Despite this neglect, they plodded on, with their characteristic clanking sounds becoming more pronounced as they became due for works overhaul, by which time they were almost invariably rough riding.

I was fortunate enough to see these engines in action on the LNER before they commenced their war service and on their return, running with their WD numbers. In 1950 they were to be among the first engines which I photographed when I took up railway photography. Over the years, despite the fact that they were the most familiar locomotive type on the East Coast main line, especially on heavy Ferme Park coal trains and return empties, I took pictures of them whenever the occasion arose.

After the war some engines were to end up far from our shores, some 2–8–0s going to Hong Kong with others working in Holland and Sweden. Examples of the 2–10–0 design were sold to Greece and Syria. Had it not been for engines that spent their working life in distant countries we would not have an example of the 2–8–0 design in this country today.

Despite many more modern locomotives being available, the last example of the 2–8–0 design was not withdrawn from British Railways until 1967. No. 90682 of Normanton was the last to be condemned. No fewer than 123 locomotives were still in service at 1 January 1967, most having completed almost twenty years with British Railways. A considerable number of the much younger Standard 9F 2–10–0s had already gone for scrap by this time. Unfortunately, no examples of these locomotives were saved for preservation.

The last example of the class, no. 90732, carried the name *Vulcan*, the nameplate being fitted on the cabside. This engine was among the first to go, being withdrawn from Frodingham in September 1962.

The WDs were well known for their clanking sounds, especially when due for a general overhaul. Here, no. 90035 approaches St Ives with a train of empties bound for March. The LNER purchased 200 engines to be set against the building programme; these became class 07, and this was one of them, LNER 3035, later no. 63035 and in February 1951 no. 90035. Its WD number was 77412. This engine remained in service until February 1966.

1.7.54

Several WD 2–8–0s undergoing general overhaul at Crewe Works, 1952. No. 90407 and no. 90059 have been completed and await the return of their tenders. These were heavy freight engines so did not remain long in this immaculate condition. No. 90407 was a New England engine, with a 35A shedplate already fitted; it finished its working life at Wakefield, being withdrawn in June 1967. It was among the last WDs in service.

12.8.52

Ex-works WD no. 90031 stands in splendid isolation in Crewe Works yard. In the background can be seen the frames and wheels of another 2–8–0, together with tenders, frames and other engine parts. No. 90031 was one of the batch purchased by the LNER and later becoming British Railways stock. It was withdrawn from New England in May 1963.

12.8.52

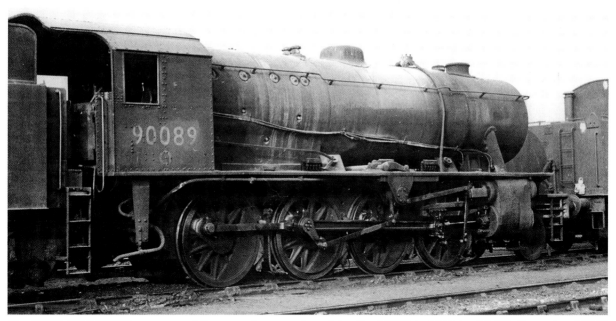

No. 90089 (WD 78527) was one of those engines purchased by the LNER in 1946 for £4,500. Becoming LNER no. 3039, its early days were spent at St Margarets Edinburgh before it moved to the north of England, where it was allocated in turn to Newport, Hull (Dairycoates) and finally Wakefield, from where it was withdrawn in January 1967. This picture was taken at Normanton.

20.3.66

There were few parts of Britain in the early fifties where you would not come across a WD 2–8–0, although those on the Southern Region did not remain long. This is no. 90119, photographed in the yard at Toton. Formerly WD 77022, it had spent some of its working life in Holland before being returned to the War Department.

4.4.54

New England was home to a considerable number of WD 2–8–0s. Here no. 90346 heads past Walton with a long train of coal empties. Note the two sets of travelling post office lineside equipment; the nearest is a dispatching point only, while the one in the distance also has a net to receive pouches from the train.

24.9.55

During the fifties WDs and later 9F 2–10–0s were the principal heavy goods engines employed south of Peterborough. Here, no. 90244 passes through Huntingdon heading a mixed freight. The train was about to be turned 'slow road', the sighting board on the signal having a small repeater arm at the back. No. 90244 ended its days at Tilbury depot from where it was condemned in August 1962.

25.10.64

Two locomotives which were used by the War Department stand side by side at Boston depot. On the left is 04 no. 63759, one of the famous Robinson Great Central Railway design, which was a Railway Operating Division locomotive in the First World War and was later taken into LNER stock. WD 2–8–0 no. 90495 (WD 78710) spent its final years at Mexborough shed, ending its working life in December 1962.

13.3.55

WD no. 90151 has a full head of steam as it nears the end of the 1 in 200 down gradient from Abbots Ripton. This New England locomotive was heading one of the many heavy coal trains to Ferme Park in London. WDs were so frequently seen at Huntingdon in the fifties that many enthusiasts paid little attention to them.

4.4.55

Track-laying in progress near Offord. WD no. 90093 of New England shed was in charge of the train carrying new rail sections. WDs were often used on this work, as were New England's J6 class 0–6–0s. This locomotive was transferred away the following year with the arrival of more Standard 9F 2–10–0s. The end of the road for this one came at Tilbury in August 1962.

30.1.55

The WDs allocated to the Western Region were easily recognisable by the top feed cover and fire irons compartment which can be seen on the footplate ahead of the cab. No. 90312, after spending several years on the Western Region, was transferred for its final year in service to Gorton. The engine is seen here shortly after a general overhaul at Oxford.

27.2.55

Two WDs modified by the Western Region pictured on a dull grey day at Woodford Halse depot, an Eastern Region depot with the shedcode 38E. No. 90676 was an Ebbw Junction locomotive; these were frequently seen here at this time, as were B16 class 4–6–0s from the North Eastern Region. The WDs were principally used on heavy mineral trains to and from South Wales.

27.3.55

Several WD 2–8–0s were allocated to Banbury during the mid-fifties, one of them being no. 90579 which is shown here in the process of being coaled. During its service on the Western Region it was allocated to several depots including two in South Wales. It ended up at Barrow Hill, from where it was withdrawn in February 1965. This engine was one of those built by the Vulcan Foundry in 1943.

24.11.54

Even in the mid-fifties many of the WDs were covered in grime. No. 90529, seen here at Oxford, was in this condition, the cabside number barely visible. Only for short time after a general works overhaul were WDs seen in reasonable condition, as goods locomotives and shunting engines seldom, if ever, received attention from cleaners.

29.4.56

WD no. 90005 of Colwick depot approaches Walton with a heavy coal train from the Nottinghamshire coal fields. This locomotive would almost certainly come off for servicing at New England although WDs worked through to March. These locomotives, although built for a comparatively short life, were to prove invaluable to British Railways. Unfortunately, one was not selected for preservation as part of the National Collection.

6.9.62

WD no. 90169 has been given the Up main from Huntingdon on its journey to Ferme Park and is going in fine style with a mixed freight. The WDs in good condition were capable of a fair turn of speed, although they were notorious for their rough riding and clanking sounds especially when in a run-down condition.

2.1.53

This is an unusual picture of WD no. 90519 of New England depot near the small sub-shed at Huntingdon East. The engine had brought the New England breakdown crane to re-rail J15 no. 65475, derailed while working a goods train. To get to the position the WD had to go through Huntingdon East station with its limited clearance, tight curves and check rails, no doubt accompanied by much squealing from the wheel flanges.

3.8.55

During the fifties the goods yards at Huntingdon were quite busy, and a J15 class 0–6–0 from Cambridge was outstationed and carried out shunting work. Wagons for onward travel were assembled near the station ready for a pick-up goods. No. 90259 was on this duty when this picture was taken. Usually this work was done by a WD or V2 class 2–6–2. The station overbridge in the background disappeared when the station was rebuilt.

2.5.53

WD no. 90158 is just starting to open up as it approaches Huntingdon station with a long train of coal empties. Ahead of it is a long 1 in 200 drag to Abbots Ripton. The locomotive was on the main line so would need to get a move on as it would not be long before the arrival of an express resulted in the train being turned 'slow road'.

2.54

New England depot was just a month away from closure when this picture of no. 90296 was taken; very few locomotives then remained at the depot, which was a mere shadow of its former self. Only a few years previously it had had more than 160 locomotives in its allocation. No. 90296 was a Doncaster engine at this time; this was also nearing the end with just nine months left in service.

6.12.64

The March to Cambridge line via St Ives was extensively used by goods trains to avoid the busy Ely route. March depot in the early fifties had a considerable allocation of WDs; these were employed on heavy freight working to Temple Mills and elsewhere. Here, no. 90442 rattles through St Ives with a mixed goods on its way to Cambridge. All traces of this railway junction have long since gone.

1.7.54

Fresh from general works overhaul, this is WD no. 90344 at its home shed, West Hartlepool. These engines looked smart after overhaul, but it was not long before they took on a work-stained appearance and became coated in grime. No. 90344 remained at West Hartlepool for another eight years before being withdrawn from service.

8.7.56

Whenever there was heavy mineral traffic there were usually also WDs. No. 90350 was one of those allocated to Thornton where it was to remain from 1948 until August 1966 when it was withdrawn. The WDs were mainly used on heavy coal trains. Next to the engine is J83 class 0–6–0T no. 68453, one of several allocated to the depot for shunting work.

23.8.55

A large number of WDs were to be found in the north of England in steam days. The London Midland Region depot at Wakefield, where this picture was taken, had no fewer than sixty-seven allocated to it in the mid-fifties, amounting to two-thirds of the shed's entire stock. Their principal work was hauling coal trains originating from collieries in the area. No. 90234 and a classmate are pictured awaiting their next duty. This particular engine ended its days at Grangemouth in November 1963.

13.5.56

Approaching St Ives station, this is WD no. 90064 heading for March with a mixed goods. At this time you could usually rely on seeing several WDs within a short time. Great Eastern 0–6–0s of classes J17, J19 and J20 were also regularly seen, plus K1 class 2–6–0s, all from March depot. In the mid-sixties this shed was home to over 160 engines, the vast majority of which were freight locomotives.

24.5.53

Coal was one of the most frequently seen loads during the fifties and sixties, not just for domestic consumption but also for industrial and locomotive purposes. Here, no. 90392 nears St Ives station with a long train of coal empties en route to March. In the mid-fifties this depot lost some of its WD allocation. This locomotive was transferred to Northampton, ending up at Gorton from where it was withdrawn in December 1964.

24.5.53

The crew of no. 90253 watch intently as the locomotive, fresh from its general overhaul, is photographed as it runs light engine through Huntingdon. The British Railways lion and wheel emblem can be clearly seen in this picture, which also illustrates the eight-wheel tenders fitted. No. 90253 spent its early years in Scotland, arriving at New England in 1950; it was to remain here until withdrawal in December 1962.

1.12.54

Shunting in progress at the north end of Huntingdon station. The bolster wagon next to the engine was normally used to carry steel. No. 90191 was based at New England for many years and was one of the best-known members of the class south of Peterborough. It was a fairly early withdrawal, going from March depot in February 1960.

26.4.54

A busy yard at Thornton as engines arrive on shed for disposal. Among them is WD no. 90534. This was at Thornton Junction shed for many years, moving to Dunfermline for its last three years in service. The WD allocation of the depot was normally around seventeen in the mid-fifties, the engines being principally employed on coal traffic.

23.8.55

Weak winter sunshine highlights the features on no. 90169 at Hitchin shed. This locomotive is in good external condition following a works overhaul. The small distinctive chimney, solid pony wheels and general workmanlike appearance are clearly illustrated. No. 90169 was a New England engine until 1962 when it went to three sheds in quick succession, Colwick, Retford and Doncaster.

3.1.54

The heavy smoke-laden atmosphere at Stratford shed on a grey November day certainly did little to help photography of no. 90732 *Vulcan*. This was the only example of the 2–8–0s to be named. The small nameplate was carried on the cabside above the number. It was a March engine at this time, and this was the only opportunity I had to photograph it.

13.11.55

Occasionally, while I was photographing at Huntingdon, a WD with a northbound coal empties would be given the main line on its journey north, as was the case with this engine, no. 90730. Ready for the long climb of 1 in 200 ahead, the engine is already going in fine style. On the left can be seen the Up line travelling post office lineside apparatus; this set was the only one on this side, with four more on the Down line.

10.3.54

Most locomotives would be shut off on the long 1 in 200 gradient to Huntingdon. Heavy goods trains were particularly careful as they were usually turned 'slow road' immediately beyond the station. This is no. 90526 heading a heavy coal train bound for Ferme Park, London. This engine had been in the north-east before its transfer to New England.

4.8.54

Another southbound coal train at Huntingdon. No effort is required from no. 90169, the long down grade giving the fireman a chance to tidy the fire and have a few minutes' rest before it would be opened up again just a half mile further on. The WDs were powerful locomotives which handled these loose-coupled freights well.

20.9.54

March shed was running down when this picture was taken, and most of the engines present were visitors from the London Midland Region. No. 90722 was a visitor from Normanton, at this time shedcode 55E. This WD soldiered on until June 1967 when it was withdrawn from that same depot. In the background is the well known landmark, March coaling tower. Widely know as 'the Wedge', it could be seen for miles over the flat Fenland landscape.

30.8.64

Despite the terrible outward appearance of no. 90345 pictured here standing in Crewe Works yard, it survived its visit and remained in service until June 1967. The first member of the class had been withdrawn in 1959. Crewe had a long association with these locomotives. Depot shedcodes were constantly changing at this time, and this engine has 55C stencilled on the smokebox door.

16.10.66

Another WD which could certainly have done with a good clean was no. 90401, photographed at March. Some 'wag' has cleaned just part of the number. The chalk inscription on the cabside referred to the locomotive being prepared for duty on 1 February 1965. No. 90401 was a visitor from Canklow, which had several sheds in South Yorkshire before withdrawal in November 1965.

7.2.65

Another picture of no. 90401 at March alongside an 8F. The shed yard at this time still contained stored engines and others which were not officially withdrawn but had not been moved for some time. No. 90401 had already been coaled and watered and was ready to work back home.

7.2.65

The shed yard at March in 1965 usually contained several 'Black Fives' and 8Fs as well as Standard class 9F 2–10–0s, all visitors. In addition there was normally one or more WD 2–8–0s to be seen, mostly in a run-down grimy condition, as was the case with no. 90647 seen here. This was a Frodingham engine and would be withdrawn within two months.

24.1.65

Late evening sunshine produced this dramatic picture of a work-stained WD at March. No. 90647 was nearly at the end of the road. Commonly known by enthusiasts as 'Dub Dees', the WDs certainly had an important place in our railway history. The investment made in 1948 by British Railways certainly paid off as the last survivors almost made it to the final year of steam.

24.1.65

Often locomotives sent to works for light or intermediate repair would emerge with just the smokebox and chimney repainted. This was the case with no. 90136, photographed at Wellingborough shed. Time was running out as the engine had just six more months in service.

8.11.64

Years of hard work on heavy freight trains resulted in the work-stained appearance of no. 90133, pictured here at York shed. The engine was allocated to Frodingham at this time, where many of the class had been drafted in to replace 04 class 2–8–0s on withdrawal. No. 90133 was to spend its final years at the depot, remaining in service until October 1965.

2.5.64

Gloucester shed with no. 90258 of Langwith present. The shed was within two months of closure, and many withdrawn engines were already to be seen in the yards, including Manor class no. 7820 *Dinmore Manor*. When the shed closed the remaining serviceable locomotives were withdrawn.

27.10.65

WD no. 90064 stands alongside one of the covered locomotive inspection sheds at March depot. These wartime relics were built to prevent glare attracting enemy aircraft to the nearby huge Whitemoor marshalling yards. No. 90064 had recently received works repairs judging from the repainted smokebox and chimney. It was a Doncaster engine in its final years and was withdrawn in April 1966.

23.3.63

Fresh from overhaul at Darlington Works, this is no. 90309, which went on to be one of the last WDs in service, being withdrawn from West Hartlepool in July 1967. Also present in the works yard at this time were two A4s, no. 60011 *Empire of India* and no. 60020 *Guillemot*, which, as might be expected, attracted much attention.

2.5.64

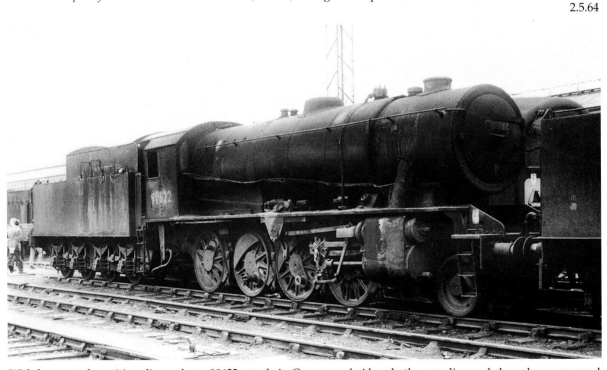

Withdrawn and awaiting disposal, no. 90622 stands in Crewe yard. Already the coupling rods have been removed and parts of the motion tied up. The final depot of this engine was Wakefield from where it was withdrawn in September 1966. Large numbers of WDs were cut up in private scrapyards. One WD 2–8–0 still survives in this country; after wartime service, it spent its final working years in Sweden.

16.10.66

WD (Austerity) class 8F 2–10–0

Introduced: Ministry of Supply Design 1943
Total taken into BR stock: 25

Principal dimensions:

Weight:	locomotive	78 tons 6 cwt
	tender	55 ton 10 cwt
Boiler pressure:		225 lb sq. in
Driving wheels:		4 ft 8.5 in
Tractive effort:		34,215 lb
Cylinders:		19 in × 28 in
Walschaerts valve gear		

Number series: 90750–90774. The last two locomotives built, nos 90773/4, both carried the name *North British*. None of the engines taken into British Railways stock has survived.

Only twenty-five of these locomotives were purchased by British Railways in 1948. Some of them had been used on lines in Britain prior to war service. The 2–8–0 wheel arrangement was favoured at that time, but all this was to change with the introduction of the Standard 9Fs in 1954.

The 2–10–0 design was intended for use where the low axle weight was an advantage, even on improvised or lightly laid track in war time. The centre coupled wheels were flangeless, which enabled the engine, despite its length, to negotiate sharp curves. At first glance there was little to distinguish between the two designs (excluding wheel arrangement), although the 2–10–0 had a larger boiler and firebox plus the addition of a rocking grate. Of the 150 built, only 7 were to remain in this country; 20 were sent to the Middle East with the remainder going to the Continent where they were to become a familiar sight in Belgium, Holland and parts of Germany. The thousandth WD to go overseas was no. 73755 *Longmoor*, which went on 9 May 1945. After working in Holland, this engine was withdrawn from Zwolle on 10 May 1951 and was then sent to Tilburg Works, being restored in WD livery and with its old number, but it never returned to England. On 29 March 1952 it was transferred to the Netherlands Railway Museum and can currently be seen at Utrecht, still carrying its commemorative nameplates surmounted by the badge of the Royal Corps of Engineers.

On their return to England those engines purchased by British Railways were allocated to the Scottish Region. Two were named, nos 90773 and 90774 both carrying the name *North British* on the side of the boiler. Withdrawals commenced in 1961 and in December 1962 the last seventeen in service were all condemned and sent for scrap.

One engine still remained at Longmoor military railway which was fortunately destined to survive into preservation. This was no. AD 600 (formerly no. 73651) *Gordon*, built in 1943. Two others which worked for Hellenic Railways (Greece) were rescued and returned to this country, with one currently on the Mid-Hants Railway, the other on the North Yorkshire Moors. Both were overhauled and returned to full working order. Although none of the WDs of either wheel arrangement taken over by British Railways survived, there are still examples of both of these very important designs which were invaluable to the war effort and did much sterling work afterwards.

One of the best locomotive sheds in Scotland for railway photography was Eastfield (Glasgow). Engine movements were continuous, not just coming onto the depot and leaving, but also the many shunting manoeuvres taking place. This was the case as a B1 4–6–0 shunted WD 2–10–0 no. 90755, a Grangemouth engine at the time, ready for its return working, under the watchful eye of a shed-based driver. No. 90755 remained in service at Grangemouth until December 1962 when it was withdrawn.

26.8.55

The twenty-five WD 2–10–0s purchased by British Railways were all based at Carlisle Kingmoor or Scottish depots. No. 90767 was a Polmadie engine when this picture was taken at its home shed. In 1961 it was moved to Motherwell. Withdrawals of the class had already started and the seventeen that still remained at the start of 1962, including no. 90767, were all withdrawn from service in that year.

26.8.55

This splendid WD 2–10–0, no. 73755, is preserved in the Dutch Railway Museum at Utrecht. This engine was the thousandth WD engine to be shipped to north-west Europe via the Dover train ferry. It crossed on 9 May 1945, the day after the war in Europe finished. On arrival it was placed in store at Calais along with other recent deliveries. It later passed to the Dutch Railways, and on withdrawal from Zwole depot in May 1951 it was overhauled at Tilburg Works and restored to its WD livery and number before becoming part of the Dutch National Collection.

6.7.89

When WD no. 73755 left our shores it carried these plates commemorating its role as the thousandth British-built locomotive to be ferried to Europe since D-Day. The plates were retained throughout its service on the Continent and are still to be seen on the locomotive in Utrecht Museum. Note the Royal Engineers badge at the top.

6.7.89

Their comparatively short working life over, a Standard 9F 2–10–0 and an 82000 series 2–6–2T await their fate in a South Wales yard. Scenes such as this were commonplace at privately owned scrapyards throughout the country in the sixties. Locomotives with just a few years in service were condemned in the headlong rush to change to diesel power. The 9Fs were one of the most successful of the Standard designs, equally at home on heavy goods, parcels or passenger services which they frequently worked in the final days of steam on the Somerset & Dorset and elsewhere at times.

25.10.65